IN NEED OF HEROES:

A FATHER'S BATTLE FROM PAIN TO PURPOSE

GREG WANBERG

IN NEED OF HEROES:

A FATHER'S BATTLE FROM PAIN TO PURPOSE

GREG WANBERG

Printed and Electronic Versions
ISBN: 978-1-956353-58-7
ISBN ebook: 978-1-956353-59-4
(Greg Wanberg/Motivation Champs)
The book was printed in the United States of America.
To order additional copies or bulk order contact the publisher, Motivation Champs Publishing. www.motivationchamps.com

ENDORSEMENTS

Greg Wanberg is a beacon of hope for individuals grappling with depression or thoughts of suicide. With the heart of a warrior, he draws from his own trials and profound experiences to provide invaluable guidance on becoming a hero for your loved ones. Having had the privilege of knowing Greg personally, I can attest that his wisdom offers profound insights into transforming past trauma into a force for positive change, not just for oneself but also for the community around him.

-John Grdina, Transformation Coach, Athletic Director,
Author, Podcast Host

Greg is a man marked by adversities; so many deep challenges, both external and internal. Yet, through it all, he has faced each one with strength, perseverance, and principled character. Greg's strength, determination, and dedication to integrity and overcoming obstacles is unmatched. It is an honor to know him and a deeper honor still to call him friend.

-Mike Dudley, Funeral Director and General Manager

Knowing Greg through some of his most pivotal years in becoming a man, strong father, and valiant leader has led me to my own great achievements in this life. Finally seeing his story in one collective and tangible place is a gratifying, full-circle experience that is truly deserving of one's attention.

This book is geared towards men, fathers, brothers, and sons but can be applied to anyone who's willing to listen, put down their strongholds, and behold something better for their life.

-Jeanette Flores, Army Wife

Greg is like a surgeon for the heart of fathers, and this book is like a scalpel in his hands. First, he identifies mental, spiritual, and emotional roots that are in dire need of exposure, recognition, and change. Then Greg attacks those roots with a passion and intensity that directly reveals his heart and character—a man of unyielding love and integrity who brings his full focus and vision to breaking men free from garbage beliefs and behaviors that ruin lives and families.

-Jesse Keeney, Paramedic & Business Owner

Greg comes from harsh circumstances, which, unfortunately, are not unique circumstances. He brings a unique and powerful perspective to the critical topics of mental health and generational cycles of pain and violence. He lays out, in unforgiving detail, what it means to him and should mean to all men to be a father and family leader determined to break destructive generational cycles. Greg is intense yet one of the purest of heart humans I have the privilege to call a friend. His genuine love for people fuels his mission; his passion is infectious.

-MSG Robert E. Mills USA, Retired, Owner of Osprey Shooting Solutions

CONTENTS

Pain travels through family trees until someone in the family faces it. Of any generational curse, ours has been running from the pain and doing as much as possible to numb it. Every dad feels the gut-wrenching blow that he could be doing better, but very few will let that pain wash over them until they figure out how to be more and give more away. Someone in your family has to step up and be the hero who will *face* the pain. Not *feel* the pain because everyone already feels it. Not *talk about* the pain because we've already given language to it. Not just *understand* the pain because we don't need all the hows and whys. No, your family needs someone who is going to face the pain and live in such a way as to be the last one in their bloodline to deal with it.

DEDICATION - TO MY KIDS, KEEP YOUR FEET

It's a dangerous business, Frodo, going out your door. You step onto the road, and if you don't keep your feet, there's no knowing where you might be swept off to.
– *J.R.R. Tolkien, The Lord of the Rings*

Dear Amara, my strong daughter, and Garrett, my favorite son,

This book is for you. My life is for you! My lifestyle is for you.

Pretty, you are my favorite girl EVER! I love you more, and I wrote it in a book before you could (so I win).

Son, you are my best team. "Friendship." You are my homie, and you have inspired me since you were a toddler.

The two of you are my world—the best parts of my life. I never cared about being happy, but I am happy with you. A lot of guys have their best moments spent partying or in sports or girls they didn't marry or something else. I pity them. Being your dad has awarded me with "the best moment of my life" over and over and over. Doing life with you the way we do is something I thought was impossible for a long, long time.

From the dangerous adventures, cussing together, teaching

you to drive at nine years old, teaching you to sweep, breaking certain rules, Charley horses, working out together, and more. You made everything I went through worth it. Thank you for letting me be your dad.

I have seen Angels. I have seen miraculous healings. I have heard the audible voice of God and many other amazing things. I've traveled the world and had a very adventurous life, but you two are the best adventure I've ever had.

What are we doing here, then?

My story, and the story that you need to hold on to, is so much more than just who I have been as a dad for you. The good things are great, but there is more to it, and if you don't listen, you are at risk of losing your way and repeating the same crap that happened to me.

It is more than me just being your dad and loving you and giving you different from what I had.

This is about who I became, what I endured, and the decisions I made along the way that led me here. I hate that phrase, "what I had to go through." It's too passive-sounding. I didn't *have* to go through anything. I had a dark pit to get out of, and I *wanted* to, which took years and tens of thousands of small decisions and a painful dedication to doing the right thing for the sake of just doing the right thing.

It's about who you will become and, more importantly, how you raise your own children. That is legacy: the impact of a man's life on his family from moment to moment and the lasting impact after he is gone. My entire goal has been the way your unborn grandchildren grow up because of what I'm doing today.

No matter what path we choose, there will be an impact. I decided that my impact would be founded on the word of God, on character, and on intimacy.

My remaining time is limited, and there are things you must know before I go. You have to learn so you can embody our family values and pass them down.

The cycle must stay broken. My role in our family was to give a new meaning to our name, to raise you in the new way, and to equip you to carry the torch forward. It was my part to break the cycle for you, and now your role is to continue this cycle for yourselves and your children.

You both know some of the stories about where I came from and what I had to do to get here. This book is about the mindset, principles, and simple actions it took for me to not be defined by what I went through *and* to become something different entirely.

The proof of my victory and faith, above and beyond anything else in life, is you two. I have lived quite an amazing life and have impacted eternity for many. But you two! You two are the proof that what God did in me and the man I chose to be is real. What we have is so much more than just a good dad, which has been hard to clearly share with other men. I wish

I could just capture what we have, like a video or something, because it would have been easier to get more dads on board!

I just want you to understand what I went through and how I did the impossible—becoming the dad you knew despite immovable odds. This is our family story, and you will have a time in life when you will need the strength, guidance, and challenge of this story to win your own battles.

I did not wake up one day as the dad you loved. I did not just magically appear as a dad who could stomach his little children calling him on his BS. This, me, who I am to you, is the result of tiny decisions, 100s of times a day, for over two decades, in the face of horrendous emotional, mental, and physical pain.

That's What You Pay For (in Garrett's voice)

There is a price for everything. Everything. If you want to be strong you cannot also be comfortable all the time. If you want to be comfortable you cannot also be strong. I wanted to be a great leader for you and others, which meant I could not also be broken.

Who I became along the way cost me tremendously. Mostly, I had to pay a price every single day of being here. Let me explain.

I wanted to go home and be with Jesus, the same way I tried to kill myself at 16 and the same way I realized at age seven that if I could just die, I'd be free of my torment. I was tired.

Especially during the seven years of hell (more on that later).

But your mother told me that my being here was the cost of living. I could go home, but if I wanted to be with her and you and do what God called me to do, then I had to stay. Staying meant enduring hell. That was a price I paid every day for five more years (more on this soon).

It took more of me than I thought I could give. That's the scary part. When life comes knocking and you have to do more than you think you can. When you have to be something you don't know how to be. When you have to act on faith for something you've never even seen.

You have to decide, maybe a million times per day, what you are going to do about it. And what can we do but keep our promises?

It takes something from you. And not usually in a nice way. Like those workouts where you cannot catch your breath, but a new round started anyway. Days when you are without hope, but people are still counting on you. In Brazilian jiu-jitsu (BJJ) you get your butt handed to you, but the match isn't over.

These are what I call pits: the cold, unpleasant places we go through when we honestly pursue growth and vision.

Funny thing is, the parts of yourself you lose in the pits are the parts you didn't want anyway. But this is only true for those who persevere in the faith and do the right thing. The sad thing is that every time we hold back, we are only protecting the very thing we hate in ourselves, the thing we would like to see die.

It comes down to growth or comfort. So we either protect our comfort and keep our same bullshit and weakness, or we go into the fire and protect our promise, and grow our character and life, and get stronger.

To be the dad you love, I chose fire. I pushed into the pain to protect my promise. I pursued God, kept my promise, fought to change, and cared more about how my life impacted others than I cared about the hell I was going through.

This Is Your Path. Ponder It, And Study It Well.

You are set up for success because your mother and I feared and served our God with our whole hearts.

But you are in grave danger of throwing it all away if you don't learn. That is what this book is for.

I love you. I believe in you. Your children and this world need what God gave you more than you will ever know. You are the hope the entire world has been waiting for.

Don't toy with your value.

You were made for glory. Now go and get it;)

-Dad

PREFACE

Society is minimizing the importance of dads while scrambling to cure the cancers of fatherlessness at the same time. In tandem, in our world right now, there is a rise in mental health issues in men and a decline in present fathers and strong families.

These are intimately related.

Since the 1970s, the number of fathers in the home has declined. Beyond fatherless homes, a home in which the dad does not live permanently, fatherlessness has mutated into dads being so consumed with work, or pleasure, or hobbies that they are unavailable. Less impact but the same effect; dads so unavailable they might as well be gone.

At that same time, mental health issues for men have risen. Not only the number of men with mental health issues but the types and severities of mental health issues.

Fatherhood has disintegrated, and mental health issues have increased. These are happening at the same time for a reason:

Something dark is trickling down through the generations, and you and I are face-to-face with it.

Here it is: the effects of fatherlessness breeding more fatherlessness.

Boys are growing up without noble identities, and they become dads who do not truly know who they are. In turn, they suffer the angst and shame of knowing they need to be more for their kids but not knowing how.

Men lack direction, understanding, and ability. These are things that come from fathers. Unless we change, we cannot give direction, understanding, or a path to our children.

You cannot give what you do not have, and this, I believe, is the reason why so many men are anxious, depressed, hating themselves, terrified, lacking confidence, are in mediocrity, in bland relationships with their wives and kids, and hooked on vices and entertainment.

Dads have a massive responsibility. Then, for me and far too many others, not having a father figure was thrown into the mix. My dad loved me with all his heart, but he didn't know *how* to love me. My dad worked hard, but he didn't know how to work through what was happening in his life in a way that he could still be my hero and excel so he could preserve our bond. No one showed him, so he didn't know how to show me. (I don't fault him for this, but this is the hard truth many of us face.)

And that's the cycle. Boys who grow up not getting what they really need from their dads eventually become dads who don't know how to fully meet the needs of their children, and those children grow up not having their needs met.

The cycle has to break. Someone has to answer the call, be the hero, and make the difference.

Guess what? If your parents were going to be the ones to do it, they would have. Are we going to wait for our children to do it, adding one more layer of generational BS over their souls and hope? Look around, man. You are the only one here who can actually make a change.

It is you and me. We are the chosen ones. Your entire family, for decades, has been waiting for a man to learn who he is and how to live well, live with purpose, break negative cycles, and bring the children onto the path. Your family has been waiting for you because you are the one who can stop the heartache, and stupidity, and selfishness.

If you are like me, you want this but feel some type of pit in your stomach because you have no freaking clue how to do it. You've looked for guidance, and now you are just waiting for the strength and opportunity to make it real.

Brother, you have the opportunity and strength you've been looking for inside you already. It has been there the entire time. Because you can choose, you can change, and because you can change, you are free.

I am a father, and I am telling you as if you were my son: *You have it inside of you, Son, that glory is already there. You can choose. You are free. Have the courage to go forward.*

Have the courage to be real about where you are.

Have the courage to believe you are capable.

Have the courage to let go of the pleasures holding you back.

Have the courage to make a stupid amount of money and still

be around your kids more than anything.

Have the courage to stop running from the pain.

Have the courage to increase your sense of worth.

Have the courage to increase your optimism about the future.

Have the courage to be different.

Have the courage to be sober.

Have the courage to endure the pain of change.

Have the courage to fight against the lies and fears in your mind.

Have the courage to see the man you needed and then live your entire life to be him.

Have the courage to follow your heart into the good thing you want for your family.

Have the courage to sacrifice the hurt for the good and the good for the great.

Have the courage to find a father figure now and get the right help.

Have the courage to accept that you must become the hero you needed so that you can give him away. If you don't, you will be condemning your kids to what you've gone through and worse.

Dads, are you ready to embark on a multigenerational, life-changing adventure?

___

WARNING: THIS BOOK WILL CHALLENGE YOU TO YOUR CORE

You will feel inspired at what is possible, embarrassed at your pity, convicted of your flaws, and regret how you've lived up to this point. I am not here to be your friend or award you for suffering. I am here to make you the man you needed because this really is a matter of life and death. You are in danger of facing your excuses. In danger of facing the pain you keep trying to hide. In danger of seeing that you, more than anyone else in your entire life, have been the most harmful to you. But you are also safe. Safe because a path forward is already marked. Safe because I believe in you. Safe because I truly understand and have made it my life's mission to help you find peace and freedom. I am here to inspire, motivate, and direct you into transformation. I am here to help you break the chains of depression and despair and the hurt that comes from not bonding with your parents. I am here to ignite a passion for growth, hope, and legacy. I am here to show you how to become the man you needed, so you can give him away.

DO NOT just read this book. Implement it. Take notes. Practice it.

In this book, you will learn the nine rules I lived by to overcome clinical depression, suicide, and psychosis to become the inspiring, badass Dad that saved his bloodline:

1. Find a new standard of truth.

2. You are loveable. Receive it.
3. Take control of your mind.
4. Decide the kind of man you want to be.
5. Love regret.
6. Develop yourself into a man.
7. Get back up Every Fuckin' Time.
8. Carry a noble burden.
9. Win their hearts.

For things to change, you must get so damn good at being a dad you admire that your wife and children are changed because of it, and the darkness will melt away.

This book will teach you how to use these nine rules to develop the direction, understanding, and ability to go from dissatisfied, lost, and hurting to powerful, meaningful, and respected.

1. Direction: know exactly who you are (rule 4) so you know exactly how to live (rule 5).
2. Understanding: discover the truth behind your life (rule 1) so you can do the deep work in your core (rule 2) and mind (rule 3) to not just get better but transform.
3. Capability: using your body, time, and mind to become the man you needed (rule 6), find the power to keep going (rule 7), turn your suffering into your purpose (rule 8), and effectively lead your family into good, lasting change (rule 9).

INTRODUCTION

This book is written to help fathers. Fathers who are depressed, discouraged, or dissatisfied with life. Fathers who didn't have a father figure but are trying to be better fathers for their children. Fathers who feel the pull in their hearts to shape a better future for their kids.

The title will be laid out in three sections, the second of which is written as a letter to my children. Writing the second part as if to my own children helped me truly capture the story and deliver it in a meaningful way.

The stories, lessons, and strategies in this book will benefit anyone battling depression. I have helped male and female teens, divorced middle-aged individuals, parents in their 50s and 60s, and even single moms. My expertise is fathers with young children because that is the story I lived and best understand, and it is where I feel most called.

We are not celebrating scars or averages, patting ourselves on the back for the hurt we've gone through, *or* for meeting the baseline expectations.

I will repeat this multiple times throughout this book: The cure for depression for dads is to get so damn good at being a dad they admire, their family is changed by it, and the darkness just melts away. Let me explain what this means:

Michael Jordan, the greatest basketball player of all time, would not allow his feelings to be hurt by people saying he cannot play ball. Why? Michael Jordan knows how good he is, and he has the championships, fame, reputation, and wealth to prove it. He will not allow untrue words from someone below him to convince him that he hasn't achieved what he actually has.

When you get so damn good at being a man you admire, imagine how your life will be. Your wife is going to desire you like never before. Your children will go crazy without you around. You will be such a man as to make their lives better, and there won't be anyone else for them to look to. They will respect you because they want to and follow you because they love you. You will be better at handling problems, leading, and serving them. All of this is beyond materials and the superficial, and it will stay true when life is great, and especially when life is difficult. More so, your children will follow your example in conduct and will teach it to their children. The results of your change will outlive you.

You will have broken the cycle of absent, unavailable, ill-equipped, or otherwise incapable fathers. Imagine how hard it will be to doubt yourself then? To believe you are hopeless, worthless, or rejected? To wonder if you have a purpose?

You may still face dark things. They just won't have anywhere to stick. You will be free.

You were made for glory. You were made for such a time as this.

———

PART I:
IN NEED OF HEROES

We make men without chests and expect from them virtue and enterprise. We laugh at honor and are shocked to find traitors in our midst.
– C.S. Lewis, The Abolition of Man

—

Fatherlessness is the pandemic of the generations and creates issues that bleed into manhood and negatively affect mental health and families.

Yet, father issues are the symptom of fatherlessness.

The Real disease is not the past but how fathers are living and fathering today.

I
DADS ARE IN TROUBLE

Do you FEEL in charge?
– Bane, The Dark Knight Rises (2012)

"Greg, do you think there are different rules for you? No one can just stop being depressed, not even you."

Working hard to heal and change, only to be trapped in a cycle of despair, is heartbreak on a whole new level. If you are like me, you still have some fight left in you (even after the hard years), and even though it hasn't been perfect, you have sincerely tried to change and overcome. It is like your heart gets sick with sadness when you fight to grow and hang on, and the darkness just circles back and smothers you again.

I sought help for over a decade and had professionals, friends, and even family members telling me that the internal pain I was carrying was a life sentence.

"You can't just make it different because you want it to be."

"You are broken from your past, and you will be fighting this the rest of your life."

"The best you can do is cope and get some good medications."

"You don't make the rules. You can't just *beat* depression."

Yes, I believed the rules were different for me, just like I believe the rules are different for you. I absolutely, with my whole heart, believed that I had a say in the kind of man I would become. Believing I had no choice in the matter of my mental health meant believing that it was forced upon me and I was powerless against it, and there was no hope in that. If there was no hope, then what was the point of living? If I didn't have a choice, then what was the point of hope? And if I didn't have hope, how could I possibly give hope to others?

And Still...

In 2022, the Mental Health Industry was estimated at $415 billion, with expectations for annual growth rates to put this industry at $570 billion by 2030. There are multiple enterprises that make up the mental health space, including technology, pharmaceuticals, and the men and women who counsel and console. In addition to multiple enterprises combining forces to impact the mental health space, we are in a society where it is increasingly more acceptable for a man to show emotion and vulnerability about his struggles and even get therapy or counseling.

We have a booming industry and an uptick of men who are invited to open up. We have the technology, drugs, medication, experts, professionals, and societal support for men to work through their inner world.

More fathers are depressed, dissatisfied with life, and lacking purpose.

Many of these dads are still lacking confidence in themselves and in the home.

And many of these dads still do not know how to control their thoughts and emotions and prevent their past and battles from inhibiting a deeper bond with their own children.

These dads have more chemical, technological, and market support than ever in the history of humanity. There is more help for dads to feel better now than ever before.

Crazy thoughts?

Voices?

Anxiety?

Terrified?

We have pills, phone apps, professionals, experiences, and more to help you not feel that way any longer.

The industry and the enterprises it is composed of are growing, but dads are still feeling lost, and the fatherless epidemic is not waning. The industry is estimated to grow by $150 BILLION in less than 10 years, and they still don't have a cure for depression for dads. How can that be?

There are reasons why more dads commit suicide at the end of their lives than early on and why, despite the booming mental health industry,dads are still in despair. There is a life-threatening discrepancy here, but before we look at that, we must talk about what depression really is.

Depression is the lack of meaning: meaningful purpose, meaningful identity, meaningful direction, and meaningful relationships. Quality of life, feeling like life matters and is worth living and that my life is something I am thankful to be part of, is the opposite of depression. Depression is the emptiness, hopelessness, sorrow, and heaviness that come from a man not knowing who he is, not seeing any meaning in the pain he has experienced, feeling his worth and identity are tainted by his experiences, and having no sense of direction and greater purpose.

Depression IS NOT the symptoms of depression: loneliness, suicidal ideation, emptiness, hopelessness, loss of pleasure, weight gain, weight loss, guilt, fixating on the past, terrified of the future, back pain, or headaches.

Overcoming depression is NOT the elimination of any of the symptoms of depression.

Overcoming depression is the right actions, thoughts, and systems employed so consistently and fervently in the midst of depression that a man's core changes. It is the pursuit and achievement of being shaped by meaning, service, and virtue instead of by circumstance, feeling, or trauma.

As with nearly all diseases, which are the result of lifestyle choices, most depression is the result of lifestyle. Men battling depression are the result of a combination of a disconnection in boyhood between him and his own dad and how he is living as a dad for his own children right now.

It is the use of mind, body, time, duty, and relationships that lead to depression or lead someone out of it.

The Statistics Are Lying

Statistics from 2022 show depression rates among men are highest from 18-25, with 14.9% of men 18-20 struggling with depression and 15.1% of men 21-25 struggling as well. From ages 26 to 34, there is a 30% decrease in men battling depression, dropping from 15.1% to 10.7%. At age 35, there is an even bigger decrease in men battling depression until the age of 54, where these rates drop from 10.7% of men to 4% of men battling depression. At age 55, there is a sudden jump back to 7.3% of men that age feeling depressed, and then the numbers start to decrease again.

Depression in men is reported to be highest from 18-25, after which significantly fewer men battle depression. At age 55, the number of men with depression jumps again before it goes back down around age 60. Did you know that more men 45 and older commit suicide than men between 18 and 24? In fact, men 75 and older have the highest suicide rate, nearly double that of any other age group of men.

There is a *massive* oversight between age 24, where the

number of men with depression decreases, to age 75, when more men kill themselves than at any other age.

STATS ARE LYING REASON #1

The statistics are lying because depression is diagnosed by the symptoms of depression. If the symptoms of depression decrease, it is said that the man is not depressed, which is why the statistics show a drop in depression. If the symptoms of depression arise or return, it is said the man is depressed, which is why we see a rise in depression later. Like putting black electrical tape over your vehicle's 'check engine light,' men are made to feel better, not made to be better. This is escapism on a generational level because as the dad feels better without really changing, the issue persists and flows down to his offspring.

STATS ARE LYING REASON #2

Many boys are not raised by good, strong men, and many young men are not mentored by good strong men. Dads are not learning in their formative years or in the midst of depression how to think, act, and live in a way that offers identity, purpose, direction, and value.

The statistics are lying because, as young men, dads got hooked on this idea of reducing the symptoms as much as possible to *feel* better without having to *be* better. What men are learning in the midst of their depression is not identity, strong morals, purpose, service, conviction, courage, personal excellence, or personal responsibility.

Through much of life, and especially depression, these young men are learning to indulge, pretend, dilute, medicate, and avoid. They either never find out or forget entirely, who they truly are and how they are supposed to live. They have taught their brains exactly how to respond to the pain, and fear, and trauma - through avoidance, pleasure, vice, or work - and like muscle memory, this has become the programming through which they approach the remainder of their life. And why wouldn't they? We've been taught to reduce the symptoms and show up anyway. They've been doing what they were told to.

The reason dads are experiencing "less" depression between ages 26 and 55 before it rears its head again is the lack of real meaning. Dads are living in such a way and finding types of meaning in their formative and at-risk years that they later realize were not meaningful at all.

They didn't find meaning. They found a very temporary, ineffective escape. Further down the road of life, the effect of those escapes and superficial meanings wear off, and they are again faced with their own emptiness, an emptiness that has grown into a brood of vipers within his own family.

Dads know. We know when we aren't what we could be, but most dads already learned to avoid problems and medicate the feelings away. Dads are learning they are "good enough" to do the bare minimum. What's worse, dads know they are negatively impacting their families but are so entrenched in learned behavior and unaware of better ways to want to change.

All the while, the beliefs, attitudes, behaviors, systems, and relationships that caused the pain in the first place are not addressed. A dad can feel wonderful about himself *and still* leave his kids with a mess that he had the power to clean up. There is a false sense of achievement that becomes a drug while the real issues continue to spread. Let me contrast the false achievement with the issues below:

1. Dad pays the bills but doesn't know how to handle the tough talks like sex, insecurity, and faith.
2. Dad has a greater reputation and respect at work or church than he does at home behind closed doors.
3. Dad was good at war, not at bonding emotionally.
4. Dad is generous, compassionate, and caring in public with strangers, but not with his wife and kids in private, at home.

Men are learning harmful or avoidant ways to think, react, and process in the midst of depression. These learned, harmful, or avoidant traits remain with them through life and cause disruption, even damage, later on.

TIME TO REFLECT

Take a moment to write answers to these questions:

1. Where has "feeling better" actually improved your life in a tangible way? What results has feeling better provided?
2. What "advice" or input have you heard that makes you feel stuck?
3. What are ways you have tried to escape the feelings, pain, or awareness of your struggle? Be specific: drugs, movies, sex, working out, your career, etc.

II
WE ARE FIXING THE WRONG PROBLEM

Nothing in all the world is more dangerous than sincere ignorance and conscientious stupidity.
– Martin Luther King, Jr.

The solutions are not working because the real problems have not been identified, which means the correct tools for the problem are not even considered. It does not matter how expensive a bandaid is or how many geniuses went into its design; a bandaid alone would never work for an arterial bleed.

Like a doctor who prescribed pain medication for internal bleeding, the world is focused on the symptom while the root cause continues to fester.

When my daughter was three, she was misbehaving like crazy: tantrums, fits, stealing, and harmful behavior. She was in regular trouble with her teachers for lashing out and not listening. She was being disciplined and punished at home multiple times a day, and we were stressed. To make it worse, she wouldn't communicate. She wouldn't tell us what the problem was.

In fact, she hardly spoke at all. Guttural noises, moans, and slurred words. This was the extent of the communication we got from her. Amara was in trouble all the time, and we were in a constant battle of loving and punishing until my brother's wife, who was studying speech pathology, told us what the problem was.

What we thought were behavior issues were actually a speech impediment and the frustration Amara had because we did not understand her. She was not able to communicate her needs, which led to her lashing out and misbehaving. The light bulb that went off was bright! We got a speech therapist and within three months, Amara was speaking in full sentences, communicating her needs, and was understood at home and school. Her behavior completely changed! So what happened?

We were attempting to fix the problem of her disobedience, obstinance, and bad behavior with punishment and correction. Really, we were trying to fix symptoms of a real problem we had not yet uncovered. She needed to be understood, but we couldn't understand her until she was able to speak. If we had continued looking at the situation only as *Amara being disobedient and misbehaving*, we would have never got the help she needed and it would have ruined her identity.

We were trying to fix the symptoms!

Tylenol cannot fix dehydration. Sex will not fix insecurities. Money doesn't cure infidelity.

Do you understand?

Dads have grown weary from the energy and effort they expend to solve symptoms while problems persist. We focus on the symptoms of depression. It is a crowded hell to see the symptom as the problem and eternally chase the proverbial tail of fixing that *problem*.

So here is the right question: what is it we are really trying to fix?

What are we trying to fix?

We need to take this topic a step beyond the dad. Look at the state of homes and families. Family values are no longer a staple in our society. Divorce rates are high. Childhood obesity is criminally high. Intellectual levels in children have plummeted. Parents are spending less and less quality time with their own children.

Fatherlessness is perpetually actualized because there is less and less social, familial, and personal pressure to be excellent as a father. We are facing perpetual consequences because children are acting on the disconnect and pain fatherlessness brings, and they are mimicking that behavior later in their own lives. Most dads today do not have a father figure to teach them how to live strong, moral, controlled lives. Many men grew up without the fatherly love and guidance they needed, and it has inhibited them from being the kind of man who could give that fatherly love and guidance at home.

This is where the limitations of the mental health industry come to a head. Medication, therapy, phone apps, and "professional" input cannot generate the identity and power a man truly needs and desires. Only a father or father figure can impart this. Dads are struggling right now because they struggled as boys, and they are passing that struggle onto their own children just as it was once passed onto them. The cycle is not breaking but festering.

So, what is the root cause of fatherlessness?

The root cause is the father. A father who was not fathered by his father now doesn't know how to father his own children. The problem is fathers are not fully capable of fathering because they were not fathered.

The root cause is dads today. The root cause of fatherlessness is you right now. Once you become a man and have children, your own pain from issues with your dad are now symptoms, too. Your daddy issues are in the past, but the effect your life has on others is happening right now.

Remember, you cannot give what you do not have. A boy who was not fathered will become a dad who doesn't know how to father.

The problem with this mental health crisis is that it is the direct result of the epidemic of fatherlessness. We collectively are trying to fix problems caused by fatherlessness by treating the symptoms of depression. It will only make things worse.

The first real problem we need to address is the number of men who do not know they are beloved sons and who, by default, are allowing that pain to shape their lives and relationships. Medication, therapy, apps, and talking cannot replace the emptiness in a man's heart that comes from not having a good, strong father to lead him. The second real problem we need to address is the number of dads today who do not have their own father figure who is capable of love, discipline, and leadership.

―――

TIME TO REFLECT

Take a moment to write answers to these questions:

1. Who is your male role model currently? Does he know what you are going through?
2. What are the problems you are focusing on that are the wrong issues to focus on?
3. Do you feel like a beloved son with a home and a father you can count on? If not, why not?

III
5 EMASCULATIONS

Emasculate verb: to physically make a male into the likeness of a woman by removing the testicles. To remove the male genitalia. To take away masculinity by depriving vigor and strength and making weak.

To be fair, it is not just the mental health industry, either. It is social media, media, entertainment, public schooling, higher education, the church, and military service (in certain regards).

There is so much of how we expect men to be, approaching help for men and addressing the mental and emotional needs of men that are making it worse.

Some of it is too sterile. Some of it is too lawless. Some of it is too focused on the self. And even still, some of it is too damn focused on positivity. Let me use Braveheart as an example.

Braveheart is the epic story of the Scottish hero, William Wallace, motivating and inspiring his kin to rise up against the King of England to reclaim Scottish freedom. Wallace leads an army to unprecedented victory. The story is passionate, emotional, and violent and speaks to the heart of men everywhere.

William Wallace took on *the* King and led an army of men to victory. Imagine the movie if William Wallace believed he should just be thankful to still be alive because someone else had it worse, and that was enough for him. Or if William Wallace tore himself down because he wasn't being a good Christian to the King, and maybe he should just "let it go" and be content.

Imagine if William Wallace had followed the wicked lords and taken a bribe from the king.

Imagine if William had tasted the bread and wine and meat from the king's table and decided to "take care of himself" and enjoy the simple pleasures.

Or, if he decided that his ambitions were too big because he was leading 100s of men to their deaths for his own ideals, so he ashamedly tucked his tail and retired into a quiet life.

Or, if William was so scared of breaking rules that he married publicly, knowing that the English lord would take Murron into his own bed.

What if William apologized to the vile soldiers who violated Murron and begged to make recompense for the inconvenience?

Imagine if William was so engrossed in eating and drinking with his pals that he didn't want to marry in the first place.

Or if William allowed his sorrow and pity to overwhelm him and he let go of all his courage, training, and passion.

Is that really the story we would want to watch? Better yet, is that the story any of us truly want for ourselves?

Hell no.

So why, then, are so many of us living small, ineffective lives? We would never want to watch a movie like that. So how in the hell have we come to living like this personally and accepting it?

No man truly wants to be clean and safe all the time. No man is satisfied and proud of himself with a rebellious, rule-breaking, or partying lifestyle. No man really, at the end of the day, wants things to be about him but would rather know how to be amazing for the people he loves. No man wants to "feel good" all the time, and that level of positivity is, in most cases, seen as pretentious and gross. There are evils and wrongs that have hurt us and hurt our loved ones by how they impacted us.

We would rather live lives of adventure and risk, following a noble code like ancient heroes and living from such a powerful sense of capability and duty that we literally cannot be stopped. All of this to slay the giants, and dragons, and hardships that would otherwise negatively impact our families and tribes.

Am I wrong? No, I'm not.

Here are five ways fathers are being emasculated. This applies to professionals in the mental health space, leaders in churches, father figures in the home, the men in the circles we keep, and more.

1. **Leaders who aren't worth following:** Men need to follow someone worth following, someone who will just tell them what to do to change. Look at the professionals we are instructed to look to. Professionals in what? In being good at being men? In leading families with integrity? In being the dad he needed and giving that dad away? No. Many professionals are so in theory or academic discipline only. How can you lead a dad to be a good, strong, loving father if you yourself are not one? You cannot. Instruction is and always has been a matter of character, and the end result of my teaching will never surpass my level of character development. This is where the mental health industry and society are screwing men over: they are trying to lead men to a place they themselves, most likely, have not been by using substances and methodologies that, by themselves, are not conducive to the nature of men. As a whole, we have forgotten to cautiously consider who we learn from and this is causing us to end up shaped by people that we don't really want to be shaped by.

2. **Too much focus on self:** Well-being vs. well-giving. No, this is not just a cute play on words. The motivation, pillars, ideology, and foundation of mental health for dads

is not empowerment for the sake of breaking cycles. More than anything, a dad battling depression and emptiness needs to be the victorious leader in his own home because this is the one true measure of his value. The pursuit of well-being, being well, is not working because what a Dad really needs and wants is to be more so he can give more, not just to feel better. A good dad cares more about being a powerful leader for his wife and kids than his own pain, and too much emphasis on himself will put him in an awkward tailspin. We have tried to remove "doing the right thing" from the mental health space and, by default, have made men less because less is demanded of them.

3. **Integrity is not a pillar of the mental health industry:** A dad knows when he is full of crap. He is woefully aware of how much better he could be doing, the excuses he is making, and how much his pain is actually blame-shifting as opposed to internal damage. The majority of the depression and despair a dad goes through could be cured by him just keeping his word to himself and eliminating the crap he regrets. The mental health industry is trying to fix the man without forcing the man to fix his self-inflicted garbage.

4. **Dads are not held accountable for what their lifestyle produces:** A dad's life behind closed doors says more about his mental health and children's future than any other factor in existence. They are trying to fix a dad's depression without correcting the thoughts, habits,

actions, friendships, and beliefs that are opening him up to depression in the first place. Lots and lots of talk about feelings and the past and mommy and daddy, and not a lot of talk about how this dad is doing the same thing to his kids and how that might be the real problem he is feeling.

5. **Square peg, round hole:** A man needs to be powerful, valuable, and capable. This requires the morally correct use of each man's mind, body, and time. We have within us the strength and opportunity we have been looking for this whole time! We have grown tired of looking outside of ourselves, and God already gave us the answers right here inside our lives. Here is yet another undeniable reason why men need much more than therapy and meds. When a man lacks physical power, his esteem is lacking because he knows he is less capable than he should be, which leads to anxiety and fear. A man neglecting control of his thoughts will converse with lies and lack identity and hope. A man who is careless with his time will be overcome with regret, knowing he could and should be doing more and bathing in the shame of not. Service and duty are hardwired by God into men and a man living only for his feelings and his goals and his preferences has opened himself up to the torment that comes with idolizing himself. Lastly, role models. Fathers not in the home, fathers not engaged or present in the home, and not having a strong male role model to help later in life. If you do not receive it you do not have it, and you cannot

give it away. You cannot give what you do not have. Men need positive male role models throughout their lives.

To help dads, we must make "help" fit into who dads were made to be.

"Help" would actually help him win the hearts and respect of his family despite having grown up in a fatherless home.

"Help" would actually make a dad more dependable and capable despite what he was going through personally.

Dads are made to be strong and powerful...

"Help" would actually give the dad the understanding and direction he needs to see clearly what is going on with him and how to turn it into fuel to be and give more to the people he loves. Feeling like your only hope is therapy or medication is a soul-sucking, deflating lie. Yet many dads just don't know there is another way.

What is missing is that the attention has been on the dad's feelings and experiences and not the dad's role in the future of his children. A dad who is empowered and chooses to be a legacy-minded leader will always have a higher quality of life than a dad who is not.

John Eldridge, author, speaker, and teacher helping men connect with their God-given masculinity, said the question of every man's heart is, "Do I have what it takes?" Any "help" we offer men that do not help them answer this question is not helping but softening and corroding in a negative way.

The only true cure for a father's depression is to get so damn good at being a father you respect that your family is better because you're around. When the father lives to be this daily, the darkness melts away because it has less to latch onto.

No amount of pills or psychotherapy can mitigate the need for true moral and masculine development. Through boyhood, adolescence, marriage, and fatherhood, the heart of a man needs connection and meaning. There is no substitute for them, and without them men are lost and tormented.

Men have a need to follow men who are worth following and to be men worth following themselves. Men have a need for a noble challenge, to be pushed out of their little comforts to meet a need that is bigger than they are. Men have a need for accountability, to be scrutinized when their beliefs and actions do not align, or for when they are living by excuses and lies.

You were no different as a boy and you are no different now. Most importantly, your sons and daughters are no different, either.

TIME TO REFLECT

Take a moment to write answers to these questions:

1. Where do you feel like you are not a man?
2. Why do you feel like you do not have what it takes? Be specific.
3. How is your pain boiling over onto your family? Be specific.
4. In what ways do you believe you are failing as a father? Give details.
5. Consider the people you are hanging out with. Are they calling you higher? Do they have what you want? Are they enabling your issues or giving you permission to wallow?

IV
WE HAVE WORK TO DO.

If ignorance is bliss, then knock the smile off my face.
– Rage Against The Machine

If we take an honest moment and look at ourselves and society, we don't need data or experts to tell us something is wrong. How many of you are guilty of any of the bullets below or know a father who is?

Let us address some of the elephants in the room now so we can be as honest as possible together. These elephants are keeping dads, wives, children, and entire communities trapped in toxic behavior, moral failure, and insecurity.

- Men who are so uncomfortable with emotion that they are incapable of expressing passion for their wives, sons, and daughters. But they can explode with passion for a sports team or act of nature.

- Men who cannot share deep things without first getting drunk. They tell everyone they're "Doing just fine" and then get drunk and confess their woes without any real change.

- Men who are so lost even their dogs are on antidepressants. They have set the bar so low for themselves that even the soulless beasts in their homes are miserable.

- Men who value sensitivity but do not microdose adversity for their own development.

- Men who value "strength" but don't value showing deep affection for their spouse and kids.

- Christian men are shaped like pears who talk about being warriors for God. Believers until physical discipline is mentioned. Warriors until getting off the couch is required. Men who want all strength to be spiritual so they don't have to put in real work.

- Men who argue about politics and change while living comfy lives of indulgence and vanity. They refuse to be self-excellent but want the accolades of the moral high ground.

- Men who pat themselves on the back for not cheating but still look at porn.

- Men who are upset with their wife's physique but aren't in shape themselves.

- Men living lives they care so little about they would find little to nothing in their own story to be inspired by. What a waste of such a precious gift, drifting moment to moment as someone they do not admire.

- Men who can work a job endlessly, without breaks or food, and take on overtime but are incapable of overtime, going hungry, or losing sleep for their wives and kids.

As loving fathers, none of us would want our sons to become the kind of men mentioned above, and moreover, we wouldn't want our daughters in relationships with or marrying these anemic men.

So why do we continue living this way? Let me tell you, brother.

We look at problems with our kids and blame our wives, problems with our physique and blame a busy schedule, and with our marriages and blame our wives or parents or the kids or something else. Our depression cannot possibly be the result of the hateful way we talk to ourselves, the debilitating expectations of life that we tolerate, or the horrid habits that are poisoning our minds, bodies, and relationships, could it?

Too many men are in bystander mode, seeing the chaos in their lives and the chaos around them, hoping someone calls the police and waiting for someone to do something.

Little urgency for moral fortitude.

Little urgency for the butterfly effect of their own choices.

Little urgency for the process of acquiring in life what they say they want.

And little urgency to actually believe what they say they believe.

We are living stories that we would not waste money on watching. This has to change.

Brothers, we were born for this time. You are the one your family has been waiting for. I love you, I believe in you.

Dads - stop playing around with your value.

Stop thinking you have enough time.

Stop trying to have your cake and eat it too.

You are too damn important to squander your own life.

We have work to do, so get up and put your shit on. We're not staying here.

TIME TO REFLECT

Take a moment to write answers to these questions:

1. Where are you undervaluing yourself?
2. Where are you wasting time?
3. What pleasures and comforts are you holding onto that are keeping you from being the man you want to be?

V
CAREFUL HOW YOU LABEL IT

As you think and believe in your heart, so you will become. If you believe you are broken, you will act broken until you really become broken.

It didn't matter what I was going through; I knew I had a choice.

I exhibited extreme symptoms of severe disorders for seven years, with much less reprieve than what was expected, even in some severe cases.

In my professional opinion, and based on my education and exposure to the clinical space, these are what I should have been diagnosed with:

Psychosis *noun*: a serious mental illness characterized by defective or lost contact with reality, often with hallucinations or delusions.

- Can be cured if treated early.

- Medication is the primary treatment.

Bipolar 1 Disorder (formerly Manic Depression) *noun*: a mental illness that causes unusual shifts in a person's mood, energy, activity levels, and concentration. These shifts can make it difficult to carry out day-to-day tasks. Bipolar 1 is defined by elevations in mood or hyperactive behaviors that last at least seven days, along with depressive episodes that last at least two weeks. This was my life for seven years.

- Not curable. Lifelong.

- Medication is the primary treatment.

I hate these labels.

Even during my college career studying psychology, counseling, and sociology, I hated the labels.

People need to make sense of what is happening. This is understandable. Pain without purpose is despair, and if I at least know there is something wrong with my brain, and I'll always be like this, at least I'm not in the dark without a clue of what the hell is happening. BUT, this response is the exact opposite of the one that will lead us forward. Instead of creating noble purpose from the struggles they face - which takes tremendous courage and work and gives REAL purpose in life - they pick up a label to explain what is going on - which takes no courage, less work, and they're stuck in their same misery over and over.

Let's paint an image

Two people are agitated because things are not organized exactly as they prefer. They both get flustered and lash out because their preference is not accommodated.

One person stays flustered and blames their OCD, then moves on. You know this isn't the first time they've behaved like this and blamed their OCD.

The other person apologizes for their attitude, asks for an expectation to be met, and is reasonable enough to compromise.

Based strictly on conduct, which person is more likely to be happier? To be capable of love and sacrifice? To achieve great things? To respect themselves more?

Both people might actually be more prone to needing a specific order of things, but there is a clear distinction between a person who is taking ownership of their behavior and a person who is blaming behavior on some other thing.

I have witnessed firsthand, 100s of times, a person pulling an issue over themselves like a blanket and staying under it by blaming their diagnosis or past or whatever for their behavior and doing nothing to change. These people were hard-pressed to develop, grow, or achieve. On the other hand, I have seen people acknowledge a struggle, own their part in it, and seek to change, and they most often succeed.

Here is the catch: they actually cannot change. If they believe they have OCD, then any behavior or attitude or struggle associated with that OCD is part of their identity, and we all instinctively know that we will not try to alter something we believe is supposed to be there. They have believed they are a thing and have changed themselves to fit it because they cannot change the thing if it is actually who they are. Are you following me?

This picture I am painting of what labels do in most cases applies to childhood issues and fatherlessness as well.

The stories we tell

If we go down the road of saying *I am* this issue or that problem or this disorder, it becomes the literal story we tell ourselves and the standard we begin to live by. All of our experiences, expectations, reactions, preferences, emotions, and thoughts are brought to heel by that label or group of labels, and we bend life to fit it.

This is something I knew instinctively, and it terrified me. It was like a chess board in my mind, on which I could see the outcome of believing certain things about myself. When I considered what I knew I was struggling with, I knew the medications I would go on and how those meds affected people. To be on meds long-term, to *need* them, and to be shaped by their side effects was scarier to me than what I was dealing with. This is why I did not submit myself to any diagnosis because I did not want to live in the prison I knew it would create for me.

I had multiple professionals provide detailed arguments as to why what I was going through could not be cured, why I needed to be on meds, and how grandiose it was of me to remain convinced that I had a choice in the matter of my mental health. I caused great offense because of this!

A few clinical professionals, professors, and family members looked down on me because I believed I had a choice. I would look at my depression and say to them, "There's something I'm doing that's causing this. It shouldn't be this bad." You'd think I slapped someone's baby at the responses I got! Yet, I knew in my heart that I had to be correct because if they were correct, it meant I didn't have a choice, and if I didn't have a choice, how could I possibly keep my promises to the fullest?

I would consider the possibility that I was just broken and needed meds and wouldn't change. Believe me, I had enough proof in life to believe it, but it made me feel worse. Normally, I at least knew it was a fight, but when I thought I didn't have a say in it, I felt more hopeless than at any other point, which discouraged me from helping others and kept me isolated at home. How does believing I am broken help me live a great life and provide an even greater life for my children?

I would get pissed and talk about how faithful I knew God was, how much I had already overcome, and how much work there was left for me to do. *"I can if I want to..."* The story that I had a choice made me feel hope and power, and those feelings spurred me to act like I was truly free even if I didn't feel it, which impacted 1,000s of people around me and made my private life better. I had the proof, but they weren't willing to see it.

I trusted I had a choice, and it has been proven again and again over time. My confidence in what I'm saying increases exponentially as I continue seeing God's way provide real results while the mental health industry becomes less and less effective for dads. Many dads I have helped were in therapy for years, trying to get results for struggles that it took me only a few months to help them get.

I have seen young men and women go from struggling to absolutely dependent on medication nearly overnight. I have seen teenagers and young adults who were fighting through mental and emotional battles, with their dignity and willpower intact, get on medication to have their wits and capabilities reduced. People who had tremendous potential have lived their past 5-15 years in some medicinal fog with their minds and souls turned to mush.

The power, peace, and freedom we keep trying to create through pills is found naturally in a noble lifestyle, morality, and strong families. You have the strength and opportunity you've been looking for *already* inside you! Have the courage to dig it up.

TIME TO REFLECT

Take a moment to write answers to these questions:

1. What labels are you blaming your behavior on?
2. Whatever these labels might be, are they really what you want for yourself? If not, why not?
3. Consider all of these you are doing to *feel better*. Are they helping you heal, grow, strengthen, wisen, and mature in all areas of life? If not, why not?

PART II:
A LIVING HELL

Beyond this place of wrath and tears
Looms but the Horror of the shade,
And yet the menace of the years
Finds and shall find me unafraid.
– William Ernest Henley, the poem Invictus

—

Who I am

and why you should listen.

VI
ORIGINS

You were such an adorable child. But you were so sad. I never understood why you were so sad.
– My Grandmother, Shirley

Dear Reader,

There is a trend of not allowing our family to see our weaknesses. I don't know where it started, but it is cancerous to all of us. We find catharsis, humility, connection, and healing when we share what is going on, so why do we not share with the people who matter most? Don't you want your kids to know what you had to go through to be who you are to them? What would you give so your kids could understand why you struggled to be everything you wanted to be for them?

As I share where I came from, you will notice I do not mention *who* did *what* to me. This is for two reasons that you must take on and understand:

1. My decisions and beliefs did more harm to me than anything or anyone else could have. With all my integrity, I believe this 100%. (This is a powerful truth that is the foundation for everything I did to be who I am today, which means that this truth is the foundation of the life you have.)

2. I have forgiven them, and I do not want to dishonor them. Whatever happened is between me and that person, not you or anyone else. Any burden or recompense I might have been owed has been released. I have decided to love them, pray for them, and yearn for them to experience love and freedom the way I have.

Below I will remove my armor and share a letter to my children, telling the story of who I was and what led me to being the father I am today. I invite you to reflect on your journey, your past, and what kept you going.

As I share my story, I hope you will consider your own story and how you want that story to end.

Truly,
-Greg

_____

Dear Amara & Garrett,

In this moment, as I wrap up the final edits for this book, it is my 38th birthday. We stayed up late last night watching a cartoon you wanted to watch and then had a slumber party together. We woke up in the same bed, and you both are drawing as I

_____

type. You are safe, you know I am here, and you know how tremendously proud I am of you.

There have been so many small ways about how I raised you that were normal to you but extraordinary for me. Because of what God did in my life and who I worked to be, I was able to create for you a home where I gave you what I had not ever received for myself. It blows my mind, and I am constantly beside myself. The cure for depression, the healing of childhood wounds, and the breaking of cycles are alive in front of me every day in our home, and I am thankful to have worked to make it real.

Childhood

"If I could just die, I wouldn't feel this any longer."

Compassion and justice are virtues I have hardly ever lacked. You have seen me act with compassion and helpfulness your entire life. From feeding the homeless with you to saving drowning kids at the pool to encouraging and helping dads.

As a small child, I loved giving food to the homeless people we'd see downtown or on the highway off-ramps. My mom used to remind me of a time I made her give money to a guy because he was hungry.

Before I was seven, I regularly took the blame and punishment for my brothers. They would do something wrong, but I would take the fall and whatever came with it. One time when I was maybe five, we were left in the car, alone for hours again, like usual. But on this particular day, there were bags of McDonald's

Happy Meals in the front seat because it was my birthday.

"Don't eat the food," we were instructed before we were left alone for hours. All four of my brothers, three of whom were younger than me, started eating. When the adults came back, hell came with them. I did not eat a bite, but I knew what could happen to my brothers so I took the blame.

"I ate it." I probably said something different, but it was more than three decades ago, so I don't remember verbatim.

The punishment came, and my birthday was canceled. I lost out on dinner and cake on my birthday as a 5-year-old, because I would rather take it than see your uncles get it. The crazy thing is, back then and still today, I don't regret it. I'm glad I took it, even though it breaks my heart that kids were treated that way.

Other than that, I do not remember much that would amount to innocence. Whatever semblance of innocence I had was gone before I turned eight. Beat out of me and rejected by my own heart because it didn't help me survive.

Life was chaos. I was taught that I was the problem. Eventually, it just stuck, and I believed it. Unfortunately, it happened at such a young age that my self-esteem and identity were molded by the conviction that life would be better if I just wasn't here.

Of course, I did not want to believe it, but I didn't know better. Like I said, I was taught. This came from my leaders, after all. The people who gave me my identity told me I was a burden, a loser, and a nobody, so why would I not believe them? I became hateful and mean, like an animal caught in a trap.

Garrett, I look at you now; how young and childlike you are. I cannot imagine you hating yourself, hurting yourself, believing that everything wrong in my life was your fault. And I sure as hell cannot imagine punishing you for my issues and abandoning you. I would pull the skin off of someone for doing to you what was done to me.

At age seven, I had already been abused, starved, locked in rooms, and more. I hated myself so vehemently that I would break into fits and punch myself in the face. I was not safe with many of the adults I was around, and my brothers were not safe with me. I was hurt, scared, and at odds with my brothers. I was a very angry young boy. I was prone to rage and would regularly berate, hit, and humiliate my brothers. I would hurt my brothers in explosive rages over small things, like Monopoly or Mario. What boggles my mind today is how much hatred I felt for myself, even as a child.

As I got older and wiser, it made perfect sense, actually. I have always had a sense of justice. Justice demands punishment for wrongdoers and wrongdoings. I was taught and believed that there was something terribly wrong with me because I made life worse for everyone else. It's simple math, really.

Me being the problem + my need for justice = destroy myself because that will make things better.

Yes, this is a messed up way for a kid to think, but this is exactly how my mind worked. I turned my need for justice against myself because I believed I was the problem, so I hurt myself and continuously put myself in situations to be punished because I believed I was a problem that needed erasing.

Even at age seven, I was emotionally exhausted. I hated who I was. People around me didn't understand what was going on with me, and many didn't seem to care. Therapists were a joke. Police wouldn't listen. I didn't have any friends. And I thought I was the problem so it never occurred to me to get help. I did not want to be mean, and scared, and angry, but I also did not know that I had a choice. Then it hit me: "If I could just die, I wouldn't feel this any longer."

I prayed to God to take away this weight of shame, anger, and fear, to be free of hating myself and being such a bad kid. The feelings did not leave me.

So I asked God to take my life instead. "If you won't take this away, then let me die."

Nothing. I felt even more alone and afraid.

"F*** you," I exploded. Gosh, my screams must have been crazy sounding through our trailer walls. Flushed with anger, face tingling, and hopelessness, I cursed God. I always knew who He was. Always. Even as I think of Jesus now, I have the same sense of communion I did back then. But when He ignored my cries, I felt defeated.

If God isn't going to help me, screw 'em.

God did not talk back to me at that moment, but the demonic did. There were dark spirits nearby and they did show themselves to me. I began opening up my heart and mind to dark, evil things.

———

And finally a sense of belonging and fascination overtook my boy's mind.

I had gone from hurt to spiritual rebellion. Again, I was seven. These things shaped much of what life would be. I took on a fascination for gore, horror movies, and anything macabre. Gory, evil depictions gave me a strange sense of excitement and belonging, so I gave my time and energy to such things until I became a teenager.

Adolescent Years

After what happened at age seven, I believed in my heart that I was just broken. I accepted that the world was worse because I was here. My heart was a breeding ground for resentment, terror, harm, and sorrow.

My desire for spiritual connections, purpose, and the macabre only grew. I used to get in trouble at home for how much I read about serial killers.

There were two instances where I tried to open up to teachers and get help.

The first was in middle school. I shared a lot of my pain and thoughts aloud, and my teacher shut me down. She was so beside herself with what was coming out of my mouth that she simply revoked my ability to share in class. She didn't hear all of it, and it was too much for her to try to help.

The second instance was in high school. I told a teacher about what was going on, what had gone on, and that I needed help. The school called the adults in my life at that time, and these adults denied everything. These adults formed lie after compelling lie about me, and when it was over, the school wanted nothing to do with me, and I was once again alone, without help. This particular night was so bad I actually cannot fully remember how bad it got for me when I got home.

I made a spiritual connection with a boy named Robbie, who introduced me to Insane Clown Posse. ICP was a horror-core rap group that was in touch with some dark, spiritual thing like I was, so there was an immediate bond of familiarity with them. I was obsessed with ICP and followed their lyrics, ideologies, and mantras religiously.

This music was a release from the torment I felt all the time. I gave my teenage years to drugs, drinking, running from the cops, and ICP. ICP was some distorted sense of belonging and direction. Drinking and drugs were great because I didn't have to feel the typical self-hatred and depression I always felt. It was so refreshing to feel something other than what I normally felt that I actually thought I'd found hope.

But then the drugs and drinking stopped taking the pain away. The music no longer relieved me. I had to find something else to numb the pain. As with any immoral thing, the pleasure and relief didn't last, and I needed more of it and to add other things to it.

Self-harm. My new drug was hurting my body.

It started with burning my skin with hot metal. I can still smell the burnt skin. See the blisters. I would burn myself at parties and little hangouts, and others thought it was cool, so they'd join in. I needed to do it so I could feel something different.

And then I graduated to cutting. Deep cuts, too. I had an old Ka-bar knife with a razor's edge. I would rake it across my shoulders and forearms and watch as the skin seemed to blossom open, folding outward. Sometimes, the cuts wouldn't even bleed right away. When they scabbed over, I would pick the scabs, which was an intensely painful process. It was a different kind of pain that I found stillness in, and it also made the scars pop.

Getting high and harming myself worked for a while. And then it didn't. Again, immoral things do not last, but I didn't want to hear it back then. I needed something else, but I wasn't going to ask God for help again. Still unaware that I had a choice, I stayed focused on destroying myself while I numbed as much pain as I could.

Amara, Garrett, I know now that I had a choice. I have always had a choice, but I had no idea what that meant back then and I believe most people really do not understand that they have a choice, too. We allow our pain, and desires, and circumstances to program us to react a certain way, not really grasping that we are the ones with the power the whole time. This is why I daily hammered into you that you always have a choice, how to make the right choice, and how to keep that choice in the face of hardship. I hope it makes sense now.

I went from gore to dark spirits, to ICP, to drugs, to crime, to self-harm. Each medication felt amazing for a time and wore off, which led to the next. But what the hell was I supposed to do now that hurting my body wasn't working anymore? To make it worse, I was as miserable on the outside as I was on the inside.

I was a terrible friend. I was untrustworthy, cowardly, and did very bad things. I was on the edge of getting kicked out of school. I couldn't hold a job, so I had no money. I was a loser, and I was tormented. I hurt people I loved. I pushed friends away. I cursed God and got in so much trouble with the cops that I was looking at jail time.

To top it all off, I ran away from home during a Colorado winter and was homeless for six months, sleeping on playgrounds and in sheds and eating snow for breakfast.

16 & Suicide

I was 16 years old, had run out of ways to cope with what I was going through, and was at the end of my rope. More than anything, I was just tired. My bones hurt from how much despair I carried, and I was terrified at the thought of growing old like this. Thoughts about all of the hurt I caused and the stupid things I'd done were on a constant loop in my mind. Again, I didn't know I had a choice, so when I looked ahead at what my future could be, all I could see was what it had been. That thought terrified me more than anything: that everything I went through would be on repeat month-to-month, year-to-year, and decade-to-decade until I died.

I really was hopeless.

That is when I remembered the revelation from when I was seven years old: "If I could die, I would not feel this any longer."

That was it. Everything else stopped working and had to be replaced with something else. Witchcraft and Buddhism took over for the fascination with gore. ICP took over for witchcraft and Buddhism. Drugs took over for ICP. Self-mutilation took over for drugs. The only logical next step was suicide. That would end the pain once and for all.

I remember wrestling with the thought in a bush. It was late at night on the way home. There was a church near home with tall bushes you could hide behind on the unlit side of the building. I sat behind one of these bushes to get high again before going home. That is where I decided I was going to end my life.

I didn't actually want to die. I just didn't want to live this life any longer. Life ahead of me was as bleak and dry as it had been so far. I had my fill, and I would not have anymore. If I couldn't have the life I wanted, then I didn't want to live at all. I was done.

When I got home, I went to my room and locked the door. I don't remember what I was thinking aside from a determination to just do it. I blocked hesitation, recalled my decision and how tired of being here I was, and knelt on my knees. Without pause or restraint, I grabbed my old knife, pressed the cold blade against my left wrist, and tensed all of the muscles in my right arm to swipe.

But I could not do it. Like trying to run in certain dreams, I wanted to move so badly, but I could not cut my own wrist. I had blocked so much of my mind from considering what was happening to keep myself from hesitating that I felt numb. That numbness left quickly, and I felt naked and humiliated.

"What a loser, right? Can't even end your own miserable life." In an instant, I went from cold and determined to enraged and heartbroken. My way out just failed, and I panicked because if I could not kill myself, it meant I was stuck here, and I didn't want to be in my here another second.

In a fit of rage, I started carving up my left forearm. I've shown you both the scars. I am not sure what I expected at the moment, but it wasn't good.

Suddenly, like a light switch flipped, I saw faces. Later, I learned it's called an open vision, where God shows you a vision instead of what your eyes should be seeing. My eyes were open, but instead of seeing the blood and the knife and my pipes and the dirty room, I saw faces. 100s and 100s of faces. They flashed by on a Rolodex. Faster, faster, and faster.

Then I heard Him. "If you choose death, they will never know Me. But if you choose life, they will know Me through you."

I broke down and cried. Not because I was relieved but because I didn't know if it was worth it. It was a strange moment of clarity but I could see what could come of it, which was good, but that meant I had to keep living, which was not good at all. I cried myself to sleep, waking up for school with dried blood on my arm.

The same experience happened the next two nights. Three nights in a row, God showed me 1,000s of faces and told me that if I chose life, they would know Him through me.

The funny thing is, and it perfectly suits who God designed me to be, is that He didn't try to save me with a promise of Heaven. He knew the way to reach me was to hit me on the justice button.

If choosing life meant they would know Him, that also meant that if I chose death, I would be robbing people of their hope. I had a massive responsibility put on my shoulders.

If I could choose life and that would result in these people knowing Him, that meant I had hope, real hope. My only other paradigm for hope was knowing that if I died, the feelings would stop.

To put it all together, I was shown that there was a way out and that other people were counting on me to find it so I could impact their lives and even show them the way.

Sobering. Sobering is the only way I can describe it. I was still, quiet, and clear throughout my entire being, and the weight of this call just sat on me.

This responsibility gave me hope and purpose. I chose life.

The next day played out like most other days. But something changed in me. The way I saw life was altered completely.

For about another year or so, I kept hanging with the same friends, getting high, and getting into trouble. But I also started going to church on purpose. It wasn't to feel better or be forgiven or be part of a group. I earnestly needed to be closer to the God who kept me from cutting my wrist, this God I had just given my life to!

All In, All out

For about a year and a half, I continued the same loser behaviors I'd enjoyed as a teenager. I was fundamentally different after that night I chose life. I was haunted by the idea that my life could count eternally for someone else, but I didn't hunger for righteousness. I was having my cake and eating it, too. I was in the place I point out and warn you about often: knowing the right answer but still failing the test.

I was a spectator! I had an incredible experience but didn't want to change. I knew what was at stake but still wanted things my way. I knew what was possible, but wanted it without paying the cost.

I was a fake Christian and a fake young man. I talked about Jesus but I was not at all living for Him. I cared more about my pleasure and feelings than I cared about what He expected of me.

But something started happening that would force me to change my life or stay the same - regret. I started regretting the dumb crap I was doing. I regretted getting high and just playing video games all the time, having no direction or bigger mission. These things started bothering the hell out of me.

Like in my early teen years, I tried to supplement it all. I tried to party harder. I got into some heavier drugs. I started sleeping around. I tried to get in the Army but backed out. I was trying to cram man-made fulfillment into a God-shaped hole, and it was terrible! I knew what I needed to change and wasn't willing to change it. I knew what I wanted but didn't have the courage to really go after it. I was tormented, and rightfully so, because I promised God my life and was still not living for Him.

More was being required of me than I was willing to give, which is a theme in every hero's story.

It all came to a head after months of this back and forth. I was at the same trailer I'd hung out at for years, getting high. It was a Sunday evening, and I was supposed to be on my way to evening service but was getting high instead. Then, that sick, regretful feeling came back up. My friends tried to convince me to stay, and I refused. I tried to convince them to go to church with me, but they refused.

In a moment of total maturity, I left. I walked away from the only friends I ever had and started walking alone to church. Then I ran.

I ran as far as my weak legs and smoke-filled lungs would carry me, which was about a quarter mile. My arrival at church, the worship service, and even the sermon were non-events. I don't recall anything about them except how humiliated I was with myself.

I was embarrassed at how I had been a spectator in my own

life, even after an encounter with God that fateful night. I hated myself for how hard it was to stop the drugs and walk away from worldly desires. I felt that God was done with me.

My pastor laughed at me when I shared my woes. "God is not done with you. He hasn't even started," Nathan told me. Before I could continue whining about how miserable I was because of the choices I was making, he told me about a dream God had given him the night before.

"The dream was about you. You were driving a school bus, and it was full of people. But you were driving straight to hell. You are going to end up in hell and take a lot of people with you unless you step up right now."

"You are going to hell and taking a lot of people with you."

"If you choose death, they will not know me."

God went all-in on me, but I had not gone all-in for Him. That night was the last night I would toy with my call. I heard the call that night when I was 16 but on this Sunday night in July, I answered it.

I quit the drugs and walked away from the only friends I had. I got a job and started working to use the passion and gifts God gave me.

My work began in the church, in the community, and across the US. I was offered a position on the leadership team at church. There were a few large mission trips I was part of, but I did mission work in our own neighborhoods every week for over

10 years, serving the homeless, mentoring others, going to the skate parks to pray and talk about Jesus.

I was completely consumed with three convictions:

1. *I needed Jesus to purify my character more than I needed air.*
2. *I had to make my life count for someone else's.*
3. *I would rather die than live a small, mediocre life. I would rather not exist than be alive and not be alive for Him.*

Garrett, Amara - I want you to remember the blood that is in your veins and not from that ridiculous fear of what issues were passed down. You have the blood of conquerors in you. I made sure of that when I stepped up and kept getting back up.

Remember who your father was and how he never stayed down.

Love,
Dad

VII

THE 7 YEARS IN HELL THAT SET ME FREE

I will show him how much he must suffer for My name's sake.
– Acts 9:16

Dear Reader,

There is more I need to share with my children. This chapter is the second part of the letter you just read.

Seven years of my life were lived in what would have amounted to a psychotic break or psychosis. These seven years came after my life had changed, which is important to understand. I had grown tremendously, healed, overcome addiction, and earned respect as a leader in my community. I was happily married, had my first child, and had even overcome a crippling fear of failure and enrolled in college. Why this is important to understand is because even after my life had changed, I had much more to go through, and it was during these seven years that I learned the nine rules I live by and teach now. It was actually these seven years, not my childhood or origin story, that forged who I am today.

This is not a story about my woes and 'how hard Greg had it.' May it never be. This is a story about how a man lived in the midst of severe mental issues and STILL became the hardcore, inspirational, loving father who saved his bloodline. How I lived in that storm shaped who I became and set in motion events and standards for our family that made the amazing life my kids have possible. The pain is the best part, but the point is how I lived in the face of it.

Reader, your story is how you faced what happened. Don't let it shape you.

Take courage,
-Greg

Dear Garrett and Amara,

It was now 2012. Your mother and I had been married for three years, Amara was born, and life was pretty good. We owned a home, I was in college, my role in the church was amazing, and I was growing as a leader in the community. I got in touch with my abilities for speaking, mentoring, and teaching, and it was during this time I learned about my gift for turning pain into purpose.

Then, one day in 2012, things were markedly worse than they ever had been. They continued getting worse and stayed that way for seven years. In fact, I do not remember a time before 2012 when my mental and emotional state was so distraught. I had plenty of issues for a long time, but there was always a type of stillness in the struggle. In 2012, there was no stillness. My mental and emotional state went into total chaos, out of my control, red-lined, and overloaded. Peace and rest left me in nearly every part of my life. Despite the many trials of my life up to this point, it had never been so terrible, so hopeless, or so disturbing.

"Worse." It started with these frantic spells. Like a panic attack or anxiety attack. I would get aggressively paranoid about other people's thoughts of me. Not strangers, either, but people I knew loved me and were rooting for me. I was constantly worried about who was going to betray me, leave me, or find a reason to reject me.

Day to day and moment to moment, my trust in the people around me would shift, and this panic would spike to the point that I often found myself unable to breathe.

I was terrified of failing. That led to a terror of making the wrong decision, which brought on a terror of doing anything at all, AND feeling guilty for nearly every decision I made. And this on no small scale. It was constant and it was louder than any other thing happening in my mind. There was not a lot of this that could be seen on the surface, but my mind was screaming constantly about what a failure I was and would be. Bear Bear, Siss, when I tell you both how important it is to not let fear shape you, this is how I know. I was under a spell of terror *about everything I did for years.*

Delusions, rather hallucinations, if we use the term psychosis. I would see, hear, and experience things that weren't real, or at least were not real, in the way I was perceiving them. Taking insecurities, for instance (lacking confidence, feeling like you're not good enough), I would hear people talking about how much they doubted me or how I was going to let them down. Here's the kicker - no one actually said anything like that to me. It was just in my head, but it was so loud that it was as if it was really said. This occurred dozens of times each day, no exaggeration.

I had people betray me, lie about me, and go behind my back. It was heartbreaking and humiliating to deal with. But here's another kicker - no one was actually betraying me. It was all in my mind, but the sensations were as if it really was happening. The fear turned into weird mental and emotional hallucinations.

I felt crazy, and it scared the piss out of me. I couldn't tell what was real a lot of the time. I had to rely on the power of will, reflect on the word of God, and ask people close to me for truth.

Decisions boiled down to principles: what was the right thing to do? Will I regret this? Does this reflect what I say I believe? What does the Bible say? What do the people I trust say?

When I tell you, Amara and Garrett, how important it is to reject any thought or feeling that does not line up with what you know to be true, this is how I know. I held on to beliefs that I never felt just because I knew they were true. It was because of how much delusion and uncertainty about what was real that I learned to consider what I was thinking, compare it to what I knew to be true and make the best, right decision I could. It was like fighting in the dark, where you only had your faith to act on, not feeling or proof or stimulation.

I have the picture of the Spartan in a storm on my wall because it reminds me of how fighting in the dark felt. Spartans were trained to fight, move, and protect each other in smoke and pitch black. They could operate at the highest level without being able to see. It is the perfect picture of overcoming despair and fear.

"If I could only die…"

Seeing death as an escape resurfaced, but this time, it was actually worse. I knew better now, but it seemed that, since my state reached a lowliness I had never been to before, the torment was my destiny, and the thought of living like this again was a nightmare I could not wake from. The need to die also intensified because of how worthless I now saw myself as. For years I served God, pursued the right thing, raised a family, and was a respected leader in the church and community, and STILL I was back in a wretched state.

What the hell is happening to me? This was a constant prayer. There was no discernable justification for what was happening to me. It defied the goodness in every other part of my life, the goodness of God, and the goodness I had produced as a man. I would cry until my eyes hurt, wail until my throat was sore, and God still did not answer.

What some people experience once in their lives, I experienced a dozen times per day for seven years. I am not bragging; it honestly baffles me. Some of the dads I've worked with have experienced intense episodes like this, and their lives halted after only a month.

I want to acknowledge how dramatic and over-the-top it must seem. I can sympathize with how someone could interpret the story so far in this way. But I assure you, this is true. There is no way I can truly articulate how depraved and disparaging this time actually was. All cleverness and brevity to describe the experience of this time simply fall short.

A man in chaos spreads chaos

There were a lot of mistakes along the way.

I nearly ran our marriage into the ground because of how chaotic I was in the home.

The people closest to me didn't have answers or understand how to help me. Yet, I needed answers badly. When they weren't able to tell me what the real problem was, I resented them for it.

At the same time, I was so proud of how I was pushing through the insanity that I grew pompous and cast shadows on those around me. I was arrogant, misguided, hurting, and inspiring. It was a mess.

My position in the church became more important to me than the two of you, Amara and Garrett. A man should never seek validation for his worth from his work, but I did. There was even a time when I cared more for being at the church than for being with either of you. It is embarrassing, but that's the truth.

The most lasting error, as far as I can tell, was that I identified with the pain. Extra attention and opportunity came up in the church because of my testimony. Extra attention and opportunity gave me a great sense of value, so I milked that cow for all it was worth. As a child, I would get loving attention for being hurt, and the same pattern occurred in adulthood, so like a hurt child, I bragged about my pain to get more attention from others.

Amara, Bears, guard your heart from wanting things to be easy. Don't go looking for trouble, and make sure not to make life harder than it has to be, but don't thirst for ease. It's like a cancer that will consume you until you no longer remember who you are.

I love you. Keep your eyes open.

Dad

VIII
THE REFINER'S FIRE

He knows where He is sending me. When He tests me, I will come out as pure as gold. For I have stayed on God's paths; I have followed His ways and not shrunk back.
– Job 23:10-11

Dear Amara & Garrett,

At the same time I was dealing with this psychosis, I was also battling a lack of confidence from the neglect and abuse I endured as a child. I did not know how to believe in myself! The stress of having to be a man without ever having been shown what that means is mind-numbing. It's like life is squeezing out of you something you just don't have. I had decades of lies that were taught to me and wounds that had not healed to work through.

At the time this next chapter started unfolding in my life, I was a man after God's heart. I had been a Christian for six years, a leader in the church for six years, and had already traveled the world to talk about Jesus and care for the broken.

Pursuing Jesus was my life. I didn't just go to church on Easter or say I believed. I worked to live it every single day. So many good things had happened, from helping people out of despair, being a father figure to the fatherless, helping young men and women face their excuses and find out what they were made of, and even witnessing miraculous healings.

Regarding the seven years of hell: What do we make of such things? Why would this happen all of a sudden to a man who was truly, with his whole heart, living for God? How could this happen to a man who was not living in sin and who had seen the face of Jesus?

To answer these questions, let me ask you different questions instead: Is God in control, or is He not? Does God not care more for our souls than for our feelings? Is pain and hardship part of His design for developing a man the right way?

Nathan was my pastor and the youth pastor of our church. Nathan's dad, Loren, was the senior pastor who took me as a spiritual son. Loren and I had common emotional and mental struggles, and we both carried a spiritual burden for radical change and for fathers stepping up in the home. My spiritual father, Loren, used to say that for those God has called for big things, the smallest flaws become big issues. "What would be like carrying a pebble for someone else will be like carrying a boulder for us. God has to break us."

It wasn't a curse; it was an opportunity.

———

It wasn't my past; it was how I decided to allow the past to shape me.

It wasn't some mental issue; it was me becoming the man who could sustain and achieve great impact.

The issues from childhood, the issues from my own flaws, and the pain I pushed on the people I loved were all about me breaking free so I could show others how.

This was about my destiny, just like your pain is about your own destiny. God was preparing me to be your dad, Sissy, and Bears, and after that, to lead other dads into true legacy. He was purging from my heart stupidity and doubt and weakness so I could be a vessel to purge others, and He was also training me at the same time.

It seemed like it was never going to stop, but neither was I. As many mistakes as I made and as impossible as those seven years seemed, I refused to give up. I held on to the vision from that night when I was 16. I held onto the dream that Nathan had. Instead of wallowing, I worked on increasing my standards and taking more responsibility for every decision. Instead of blaming, I got help to process and forgive the people who hurt me.

I just got really good at getting back up after every failure and deciding that I had some fight left in me. I know my story is inspiring, and it should be, but for me, I was just stubborn. I would not allow anything or anyone to tell me that total change, total peace, and total breakthrough were not in the cards for me.

Garrett, Amara, get good at getting back up. Force your minds to see the truth.

Remember who you are.

Love, Dad

When everything changed

Dear Reader,

There is a consequence of fatherless and unavailable-father homes that are downright scientific. Boys from broken homes are more insecure, more likely to be poor, more likely to struggle with confidence, and more likely to get into serious trouble. There is something pure and immovable in a young man who had a good, strong father and did not stray from what his father taught him. There is something clear and incorruptible in a man who had the love of his mother. I had neither, and I was the poster boy for the negative outcome.

I invested the last 21 years of my life in developing myself and documenting what worked to reduce depression, rewire my mind, and give me control over my emotions. More than half of my life has been focused on a single mission, and all of my energy and effort has gone toward becoming the kind of man who could achieve and sustain the mission.

In the last two decades, I have taught 1000s that in order to have what you've never had, you must become what you've never been. I was chasing peace I never had by trying to not feel so bad instead of putting all of my effort into being the leader I needed so I could have peace. Throughout this hell, I was able to see this more clearly, and eventually, we hit a tipping point that paid off.

In 2017, due to rapid events, I stepped down from my position at church. I was inoperable as a leader because of what I was going through, and it was causing issues with the team. I let go of the vision I had at 16. For the first time in my life, I was willing to let go of the need to feel better and have a validating position. I deliberately chose to "stop caring so much about other peoples' kids more than I cared about my own." In 2018, we moved on from the church we had been in for nearly half my life.

I was done trying so hard to be a good Christian instead of a good, strong dad. It was time to just be a good dad.

Finally, after all the years of fighting and training, I had my priorities right. My passion, intensity, focus, and mission-mindedness remained, but was reserved for my kids alone.

That simple shift of focus - to be better as a man for my wife and kids - changed things nearly overnight. More than the years of counseling, years of striving and praying, and the years of service in the church, what finally worked was just getting better at being a man for them.

I was trying to fill a gap in my heart by being important to God and others so that I could believe I was valuable and important, hoping that it would benefit them. When I just improved as a man in private so I could do more for them, I actually aligned myself with God's law in such a way that the darkness fled. I started caring more about being a better dad than I cared about feeling better, getting answers for the struggle, or being free of it. And that is what brought the healing and peace I was anxious for the entire time!

Let me sum it up like this: The only true cure for me was getting so damn good at being a dad I respected so I could give more to my wife and kids, and when I saw the improvement for them, the despair melted away.

I took the years of perseverance, skills, faith, and lessons and just applied them to fatherhood behind closed doors at home and found what I had been looking for. I had been building the character, virtue, and mindset of the man I knew I was made to be. The foundation was laid, and with this shift of focus, I turned the scars and lessons into a repeatable system and have never looked back!

The lessons from the pit

I learned nine rules in the pit that, when applied to my private life and fatherhood, are what healed me and changed our lives.

No matter how bad the storm inside me was, how badly I screwed up, or how hopeless it all seemed, these rules gave me direction, understanding, and actionable steps to keep growing and moving forward. I just turned the nine rules into a system I could easily repeat in private, and that is how

I changed our family and overcame depression.

The system is composed of nine rules built on the foundation of mind (correct use of thought and expectation), body (correct use of the body and will), and time (correct use of lifestyle and private life).

These nine rules made me who I am and what I now teach to dads so they, too, can overcome depression, become powerful men, be the respected leaders in their homes, and be the heroes their kids hoped for.

It's time to get up.

-Greg

PART III:
THE HARD ROAD FORWARD

Enter by the narrow gate; for wide is the gate and broad is the way that leads to destruction, and there are many who go in by it. Because narrow is the gate and difficult is the way which leads to life, and there are few who find it.
– Matthew 7:13-14

—

The nine rules that will give you the accuracy and skill to

secure lasting hope, change, and direction

for yourself and the next three generations of your bloodline.

IX
RULE ONE:
FIND A NEW STANDARD OF TRUTH

> Don't waste your time looking back.
> You're not going that way.
> *– Ragnar Lothbrook, Vikings*

Greg, you are an idiot and a loser. *I tell myself I am an idiot and a loser. I behave like the idiot and loser I think I am.* See, Greg is acting like an idiot and a loser. Greg, you are an idiot and a loser…

Greg, you are a failure. *I tell myself I am a failure. I behave like the failure I think I am.* See, Greg is acting like a failure. Greg, you are a failure…

Greg, you are the reason for all of our problems. *I tell myself I am the reason for all of their problems. I behave like a problem and add more problems to their plate.* See, Greg is just adding to our problems. Greg, you are the reason for all of our problems…

Greg, my life is unhappy because of you...

Greg, you are a monster...

Greg, all you do is mess things up...

Greg, it would be better if you weren't here at all...

Greg, how could that dream possibly come true for you...

These are a few of the death loops my mind was stuck in since before I was seven years old. We all have these loops, for good or bad: believe something and act on it, which makes it real and proves what you believed, which compels you to act on it, which makes it real and proves the belief so you are even more compelled to act on it...See what I mean?

It's no wonder dads with depression also have low confidence; just look at how we speak to ourselves.

The lies we believed

As a child, I took on the negative, hurtful things that were said about me. Because I heard them from people who were there to lead me, I believed in what they were saying. Because I believed what they were saying, I would repeat them to myself and then behave in such a way as to prove that the negative things they said about me were true. And when I acted in a way to prove I was the thing they said I was, they would respond like, "See. I knew it." And then they would say it again.

I allowed the words of others to become my standard of truth. It was a choice, my choice. Like I have said many times, I cannot blame them for what I did because my decisions and beliefs did more harm to me than what anyone else could have done to me.

This is one of the most beautiful, powerful truths you will ever learn, sown into the fabric of everything God created. Yet, people find the pain of this truth too much to bear, and they run from it. This is why they have stayed the same, and I continue to improve.

Brother, see the hope in the pain: If *this was* your choice, then you could just choose something else, right? Correct.

But it will not be enough to think happier thoughts. One set of truths brought destruction and misery, so you will need a whole new standard of truth to find freedom, meaning, and strength.

For better or worse, beliefs shape us in three key areas: 1). What we believe about God, which shapes our understanding of life and what happens to us. 2). What we believe about the future, which shapes what we believe we are capable of. 3). What we believe about ourselves, which shapes what we think we are worth and, ultimately what we are willing to receive.

When I got involved in the church, started reading my Bible, and had good, strong people speaking into my life, the contention really set in. I was reading and hearing things that were the polar opposite of what I had already chosen to believe. It was not just switching from one idea to another. It was a complete identity overhaul.

My experiences, mental state, emotional state, and upbringing were the total opposite of the truth I started learning. When you come upon truths and affirmations that contradict your current belief system, you have a major question to answer: What are you going to do about it? Believe what you were taught as a child because you have proof to affirm it? Or commit to a new belief you have zero proof of that can get you what you really want?

The conundrum

Our problem is that we can only believe one thing, really. We can only believe one thing actively, in the moment, because it is impossible to commit to two conflicting ideals at the exact same moment in time.

To have a new life, you must change, and in order to change, you must learn to live according to a new set of beliefs. That means, moment to moment, you are going to oppose every thought, experience, and emotion that does not line up with your new beliefs, you are going to pray to be delivered from the beliefs that are not Godly, and you are going to base your behavior and choices on the new belief.

Remember that most of my time as a young Christian was lived in a storm of psychosis and torment. It was hard and nearly impossible at times for me to tell what was real. Even though I walked with God, my belief system did not agree

---

with Him. I hated myself, was terrified of failure, and believed at all times that I was doing something wrong.

My saving grace was that I was smart enough to know that I could not trust what I was hearing and experiencing inside myself and humble enough to ask for help. Here are three strategies I used to tear down and build up new beliefs and become the father my kids admire.

STRATEGY 1: WHAT DOES THE BIBLE SAY?

If the Bible says it, then it is true, which means everything else is false. This takes faith because we have to be willing to let go of what we see, don't see, feel, don't feel, want, or don't want based on what is in the Bible.

Again, this is why faith is a fight. We must use our minds to hold onto something that goes against what has happened or is happening. We must also use what the Bible teaches so we know what to anticipate, especially if fear is telling us a different story.

Here are a few of the Biblical beliefs I held on to because they offered a promise that helped me get out of the hell I was going through. :

- "Many are called, and few are chosen." (Matthew 22:14) I am not a loser because God has called me by name.

- "My perfect peace I give to you…Do not let your heart be troubled." (John 14:27) I don't have to be afraid of how crazy my mind and thoughts are because Jesus has peace for me.

- "I have been young, and now am old; yet have I not seen the righteous forsaken, nor his children begging bread." (Psalms 37:25) My future is exciting and worth getting to because I am a man of God, and He does not abandon His people.

These might seem overly simple, but simple verses and quotes like these were such antipodes of what I had believed since childhood that believing them forced me to change.

––––––

APPLY THIS TODAY

1. Find a Bible verse that addresses a fear, negative thought, or insecurity you are having. Write down the negative thing - *fear* - and next to it, write the verse. ***Make a list.*** Now, when you feel or think that negative crap, you have a list to refer to immediately to redirect your mind.
2. Formulate a truth anchor to oppose lies and strengthen your mind using this format: I am not/will not [insert negative thought or thing you're afraid of] because [paraphrase Bible verse in your own words]. *(I have given multiple examples above for you to refer to).*

STRATEGY 2: DO I WANT TO BELIEVE THIS?

It's decision time.

Do I want the full outcome of this belief?

Do I want this to be true?

Very powerful; very effective.

Do I want to believe this?

I know that I believed I was going to fail because I was a loser and always had been a loser.

But do I want to keep believing it?

Challenging beliefs and thoughts is critical. Ask the right questions, and you will find the right answers.

The thoughts and feelings are there, but do you *want* it to be true? Yes or no?

———

APPLY THIS TODAY

1. What thoughts and beliefs are in your mind that you do not want to be there? Write them down.
2. What do you *want* to believe instead? Write it down.
3. Talk yourself through your answers to 1 and 2.

STRATEGY 3: WHAT DO THE PEOPLE I KNOW AND TRUST SAY?

The circle you keep is a precursor for destiny, meaning that the people you keep around shape your future as much as your beliefs will.

As a new Christian, I surrounded myself with people who believed in and pursued Jesus like I did. When the psychotic episode started, I kept these people around me. This made sure that I was not alone on my journey, that I had plenty of people to lean on, and, most importantly, that I had honest people who would tell me the truth.

You have a powerful calling in your life.

There is a way through this and you will find it.

We love you.

This will end and you will be free forever because Jesus already won, and you belong to Him.

It did not matter whether I felt like what they were saying was true. I trusted that these men and women would not lie and that they also feared God, so their words must be true. Now, I made my thoughts and emotions bow down to the words of my friends.

APPLY THIS TODAY

1. Share a fear or negative thought with someone you trust and ask them for encouragement or positive feedback.
    a. Ask them to send it in the form of a text message, direct message, email, or written message.
    b. Do not put this in your words. Let it be their words.
2. Listen for any other fears or negative thoughts that might come up.
3. Create a truth anchor using the words of people you trust.

DEBRIEF - A NEW STANDARD OF TRUTH

- Until and unless you are willing to sacrifice your feelings, thoughts, and pain for a new belief system, you will be stuck in the negative cycles you are trying to get away from.

- Break the mental death loop by replacing lies with truth and acting on it.

- Create your truth anchors using the formula above and force your thoughts to follow them.

- Virtually every thought that brings emotions of hopelessness or worthlessness is a lie.

- The truth is unchanging and infinite, but we are temporary and finite. As you progress through life, newer truths are needed to continue to grow. Like leveling up in a game unlocks a new level that provides a new tool to advance to a newer level, so too is it with life. Sometimes, you return to a previously known truth to learn it at a deeper level. Never overlook the basics.

X
RULE TWO:
YOU ARE LOVEABLE. RECEIVE IT

**Your strength as a man starts with you knowing you
are irreplaceable to God. You are a beloved son who
cannot ever be replaced, will not ever be abandoned, and
will always have a Father to call on. That is where your
strength comes from.**
– Mike Dudley

As I tried to walk out of the room, my wife, Judy, stood in the doorway and braced herself. I was melting down, but when she tried to hug and comfort me, I pulled away and attempted to flee the room.

She was tired of me shutting her out.

"You keep whining about how you don't feel loved, but then I try to love you, and you pull away. You can't have it both ways, Greg."

This is where we start.

This is not a joke, brother. This ain't Hallmark, and I'm not here to smooch your booboo. God loves you. He does now, and He always has. You can be replaced at every single level of life except in who you are as a son. Your wife can find a new man; your children can find a new male role model. Your boss, friends, family, church, neighbors, and creditors can all find someone to take your spot.

This is the truth you've been hoping for: you are an irreplaceable son of God.

This allows you to work hard, develop yourself, and achieve great things from a place of identity and not a place of needing approval.

This quenches the need for belonging and assurance, alleviating two of the most common fears: rejection and failure.

Men have innate worth and earned worth. Earned worth is the value we amass by the value we bring to the people around us, which is replaceable and temporary.

Innate worth, on the other hand, is the value I have just because I exist. No matter how poorly I do, I cannot be less valuable. No matter how great I do I cannot be more valuable.

Just because I live, I am loveable.

Just because I live, I am valuable.

Even when you screw up. Even when you fail. Even when you don't get the job, forget the bill, lose your temper. Even if you hurt someone you love or break the law.

You are still lovable just because God created you.

You have to get it into your heart that you are loved and lovable. Every other thing in this book is worthless if you do not proceed with a willingness to receive love and a belief that your life is valuable just because you exist. Every skill set, self-help, mindset, and mastery book in the world cannot compensate for a man's empty heart.

Everything you've battled has, in one way or another, attempted to minimize your sense of worth or convince you that you are not valuable because of this or because of that. That is because your knowledge, receptivity, and faith in being loveable are the door to everything else.

You love your family. You love people. You want to love them more, do better for them, and be more to them. Brother, you cannot give what you do not have. And that is a good thing.

Imagine if you had to love but were not made to *be* loved. Screw that. You are not a robot.

You will change things for your family forever, but that is not why you are important. You are the hero your family has been waiting for, but that isn't your core identity. You will go in front of your children and learn the hard way what they will learn for free - that they are loved and valuable - but that is not your primary function.

It is our glory to fix a broken pattern, but you are not a slave, a robot, a tool, or a drone. Your belief that you are loved is not about you increasing your ability to be a better man. If that were the case, we would be repeating the same cycles without imposing *real* change.

This is just about you knowing that you are lovable. This is about you opening up that wounded place in your heart, believing that you are a son of God, and allowing His love, not your performance, to lift you up. This will set you free, yes.

Stop blocking their love

The true issue we have is that we allow hurt, trauma, issues from the past, and other people to convince us that we may not be lovable or that we at least are not lovable at this moment because we screwed something up or came up short or didn't do a good enough job.

We block love by not asking for it.

We block love by doubting it in our minds.

We block love by pulling away when our wives and others attempt to share it with us.

We block love by waiting until we think we did good enough to receive it.

Receiving love, support, and blessings fills me up so I can actually give more. We do it backward, trying to do better and work and hustle to be valuable, constantly chasing that dragon. Looking for love in every place, we repeatedly lose it. Having our productivity, wealth, and success as the only basis of worth.

Another way we are blocking love is by reacting like an animal caught in a trap instead of an adult designed for connection. To connect, we must remain vulnerable and present, but pain and hardship push us into defense or survival orientation, where we become invulnerable in one of three ways. Sometimes, we run to the first thing that makes us feel good like a dog focused on a treat. Or we might get angry and bite, bark, or snip, like a dog that is poorly trained. Other times, we might let the big bad feelings dominate us while we tuck our tail and freeze. Animals can know they are loved in one moment and completely disregard it the next.

We cannot trade the knowledge of being loved or the openness to receive love for anything. Not anything. I had to make a skill out of separating the thoughts and emotions I was having from my perceptions about myself and life. This was one of the hardest skills I've ever had to learn, but because I learned it, I am at peace with myself. It is like wearing a glove to pick up dog poop. Yeah you can feel the squish, the warmth, and you can smell it, but it isn't actually touching you.

Blocking love because I don't feel loveable or because I am too proud to need it limits me as a man at the core of my being. When I reject love, in thought or in action, I might as well be taking the little boy version of myself and locking him in a dark room without food and leaving him to rot. Trust me,

I've been locked in a room as a child, and it is horrible.

Stop waiting to be perfect to receive love. If you wait to receive love until you think you are worthy, you will never receive it, and you will never be free.

A son knows he is loved all the time and stays open to it. A son responds to pain with vulnerability, humility, and virtue. He doesn't pretend he is not hurting. He doesn't run to vices, distractions, or entertainment to self-medicate. He doesn't wallow in it or let go of the knowledge of it, either. He is able to understand that he is hurting and responds like a beloved member of a team, holding onto the truth and leaning on the family around him to sort it out.

A son stays open to love, even in pain, by looking to his dad as a reaction to all things. Your willingness to stay vulnerable and believe that you are an irreplaceable son is your gateway to healing and freedom.

APPLY THIS TODAY

1. Get vulnerable:
   a. Not just sharing your pain or embracing emotion but forcing your heart to stay open even if you are struggling, doubting your worth,
   b. You can master self-development, but without love, you are still lost and without hope.
   c. Of the most important people in your life right now,

whose love is it hardest to trust or receive either on a regular basis or when you are hurting?

    i.   Let that person know that you appreciate their love for you.

    ii. Be honest with them that it is hard to stay vulnerable. However cheesy this might seem, you need these types of honest and vulnerable conversations, and this is your moment to break the cycle.

2. Burn the ship:

    a. Write down the events that convinced you you are not lovable. *Dad never said it. Mother said the opposite. Heartbreak later in life. Failing to do something right and getting shunned for it.* Write them down.

    b. Forgive those who hurt you for the specific hurt on the list. Get a trusted friend or mentor to work through these with.

        i.   Acknowledge the hurt and who it came from.

        ii. Example: Dad, I needed to know that you loved me, and you didn't know how to show me. It made me think I wasn't loveable. I now see that I am loveable, and I forgive you for not showing me love.

    c. Take ownership and apologize to God, yourself, and your family for holding onto a hurtful belief.

        i.   We hurt ourselves and those around us by believing harmful things about ourselves.

        ii. Making this right by repenting is imperative and healing cannot take place without this step.

d. Burn the list. Run through this process and burn the list of hurts, signifying that you are no longer allowing yourself to be defined by what happened on the list.

3. Be kind to yourself:

a. Commit to a daily habit of gratitude. Gratitude connects you at a deeper emotional level and unlocks creative power, which you will need later.

b. Write four things from the last 24 hours you are grateful for each day.

i. Three things that made you happy. Something positive that brought positive emotions and thoughts.

ii. One thing you are thankful for about yourself. You must start acknowledging yourself and giving yourself credit. Thank yourself for anything you do that is noble, brave, disciplined, meaningful, or that progressed you toward a goal.

DEBRIEF - YOU ARE LOVEABLE

- Dads, this isn't a license to be weak or have bad character, to screw up or let your emotions control you. Honestly, people have a license to do that anyway and the men who really make a difference are the ones that understand that being loveable doesn't give them an excuse to be a coward.

- You are a fool if you continue living from this idea that "I can love others but don't need to accept love for myself."

- You cannot outwork the unmet love needs from boyhood. When you stop hiding and let good people love you, that little boy can heal.

- Allowing yourself to be loved allows you to truly raise the standards you have for yourself and thrive.

- This is not about you being good enough and just working for others. Your life is also worth living just because you exist.

XI
RULE THREE:
TAKE CONTROL OF YOUR MIND

**And though calamities have crossed thee, and misery
been heaped on thy head,
Yet ills that never happened, have chiefly made thee
wretched.**
– Martin Farquhar Tupper, Of Anticipation

Animals cannot reason. Like our puppy, who was terrified of the sound of our shotgun dry-cycling. He heard a sound he didn't like and reacted in fear. The shotgun was unloaded, it was not shot around him, and he was completely safe. But he is a beast with an animal brain. He cannot consider the points about safety and calm himself down. He cannot reason and cannot take in more information and make a better decision. He doesn't reason because he is an animal. But you are not an animal. You are a person.

What sets you apart from animals is that you have dominion over your thoughts. There is no thought occupying your mind that you did not give permission to be there. At every point of your existence, you can think about what you are thinking about, strike down thoughts that do not serve you, and implant new thoughts into your mind to change the way your brain works.

You think your mind works the way it does because of what happened to you, but it's actually because of how you allowed what happened to shape you. Your mind is only doing what you allow it to.

But my dad...

But my teachers...

But my emotions...

...You don't understand.

I know what hell is, and I will tell you with complete conviction and truth - what you chose to think and believe has done more harm than anything else that happened to you.

What about when we are terrified? Hopeless? Feeling worthless? Hating ourselves? Doubting that things will work out? You had a thought based on an experience or perception, but that thought stayed because you turned it into a story about who you are and what life is, has, and will be like.

People have it completely backward.

They think that their minds are tormented and damaged because of the bad things that happened to them. People are ruining their own lives by believing harmful and deceitful thoughts and blaming it on their past.

I believed I was a terrible person, ruining life for my family and friends because that is what I was taught as a child. As a child, I was told I was the reason for the family's issues, treated like a reject, and used as the physical and emotional punching bag.

I would pray and beg for things in my head to change. I hated how loud, spastic, and panicked my mind was, and for a long time, I was in and out of the loop of waiting for my mind to just get better and praying it would. It was a mosquito, of all things, that taught me how much of my panic was my fault.

There was a mosquito buzzing around my head, and I was getting mad. Not annoyed, but emotional, angry. I was cursing the damn bug out loud, swatting and fussing. Then it hit me. "Really? You're acting like a baby because of a bug?" I was getting worked up trying to swat a bug away from my head and was losing control of my emotions because I was irritated that the bug wouldn't leave me alone. My reaction to the bug was the exact reaction I had to the irritation in my mind.

I was irritated at what I was thinking and feeling on a daily basis, but my panic came because I was working myself into a fit, trying to swat them away. I allowed them to bother me because I wasn't controlling my thoughts.

I was relieved and embarrassed at the same time. It took

an issue I thought was massive - the volume of my fear and self-hate - and reduced it to a manageable level, but I was embarrassed knowing how much of my precious time I'd wasted complaining and worrying about thoughts.

I was dying to overcome what I was going through and was holding myself back the entire time because I put more energy into getting those damn mosquitos away from me than I put into taking back the control that would allow me to overcome.

Overcoming is a battle of controlling the mind. Controlling the mind is blue-collar work, and this is what that work looks like:

- Take responsibility for your mind: nothing can be in your mind that you don't want there. Nothing can stay unless you let it. Including the good. You can reject the good as much as you soak in the bad.

- Think about what you are thinking about: *"Do I even agree with this thought?" "Do I want to think this thought?" "Why am I thinking that?"*

- Challenge your thoughts: do they line up with what I know is true? Do these thoughts support me in accomplishing noble goals? Do these thoughts agree with what God has said about me? If not, they are an enemy and need to be struck down and replaced. If so, they need to be exaggerated and enhanced.

Rumination

Rumination is an obsessive, mental preoccupation. To think deeply about a thing. Rumination, being laser-focused on our struggle, negative thoughts, and pain, is a primary symptom of depression and one of the most powerful and crippling parts of depression.

Rumination is heavy but it's nothing, silent but piercingly loud, and painful but numb. It is a terrible experience, but it is a circumstance we do have control over.

Our minds will be occupied, whether passively through entertainment, through misdirection in worry, fear, shame, and self-examination, or through focus on faith, will, and practical analysis.

Focus is the light in the dark for dads in depression. Directing your thoughts toward optimism, truth, virtue, and noble goals alleviates the pressure of rumination.

Rumination is the opposite of valor, which is why so many motivational quotes centered around athleticism and war speak closely to people battling depression.

APPLY THIS TODAY

You are not cursed to ruminate. By redirecting and controlling your thoughts and focus, you can create mental peace, emotional stability, and inspiration.

To take control of my mind, I developed the Defensive Mental Action (DMA). These six prompts are the #1 tool I used when negative thoughts and emotions were getting loud. They kept me grounded so I could act like a man I respect and not like a fool I despise. Apply this to any wave of negative emotion or thought—feeling hopeless or hating yourself, fighting with the wife, kids driving you crazy, angry with the boss, or stressed about a big goal.

1. **What am I feeling?** Give language to what you are feeling at this moment. Keep it matter of fact, not accusatory toward you or anyone else (*I feel...* instead of *I am...* or *They did/are...*). This gives your enemy a face.
    a. Example: I am feeling angry and scared because I don't think I am ever going to change.
        i. Do not exaggerate or minimize what you are feeling.
        ii. Do not give many words to it. Simple, concise labels.
2. **What dark thing did I just let in?** Negative emotions are nearly always the immediate result of negative thoughts. You let something bad in, and now it is screwing with you. This helps you be responsible for what is going on inside you.
    a. Example: I listened to a thought that said I will never change.
        i. You experience the emotions and results of the thoughts you allow in your mind.
        ii. I have only ever seen noble, Godly thoughts invite negative emotions in three ways: 1). There

is sin that is not being confessed or repented of. 2). We are so programmed against the truth that the truth actually hurts. 3). When we are in the place of weeping and teeth gnashing from lack of faith or inaction.

3. **What do I know to be true?** Gird up your loins, man. In other words, find your balls. You know that what you are feeling is not true. The truth sets you free. So what is true?

   a. Example: Diligence pays off. God loves me and called me by name. I have a choice, which means I can make the right choice. No men of God have ever been stuck or forsaken. God is with me where I go.

      i. What is the Biblical, historical, or experiential proof that we know what we are feeling is not true?

4. **Who am I?** Remind yourself who you are and who you are not. Lean on your vision. Use this formula: I know *[negative feeling or thought]* is a lie because I am/have *[truth]*.

   a. Example: I know *these hopeless emotions* are a lie because I am *a man of God, and He will not lead me astray.*

      i. You should be angry. Something is trying to mess up your life and family and enslave you to a lie.

         i. Speak with fervor and passion.

5. **If I believe the lie and negative emotions, what will that keep me from doing?** It is keeping you from doing something or being something to someone else.

   a. Example: Feeling like I'm never going to change

makes me want to avoid my wife and kids.

  i. Because this isn't about how you feel, these lies and the emotions they bring are working to keep you from fulfilling your role in one way or another.

  ii. Flip the situation around: if I listen to this emotion, what will that keep me from doing?

6. **Get to work.** You have identified what is going on inside you, then recall what you know to be true and who you believe you are. Now, you need to use it.

 a. Example: I am going to splash water on my face, put my phone down, and go be with my family.

  i. Acting on faith and virtue heals, protects, directs, and emboldens us.

  ii. This flips #5 around: the thing that these emotions would keep me from doing is the exact thing I need to be doing right now.

  iii. I have identified the negative feelings and acknowledged what dark things I let in my own mind. I have held on to what I know to be true and who I believe I am. Now I need to act on this information as swiftly as possible.

DEBRIEF - CONTROL YOUR MIND

- Dads, when you get better at controlling your mind and directing your thoughts, your emotions control you less. Drive your mind, drive your life.

- Focus your mind on what you know is true and break away from the weight of rumination.

- Looking at things after the fact and thinking through them is just like practice. This will help you get better at handling situations quicker and defending your mind against lies down the road.

- It is not the presence of negative or overwhelming feelings that is your problem, but your lack of training in how to handle them.

- The road to redemption is paved with new thoughts, new beliefs, and a new mind.

XI
RULE FOUR:
DECIDE THE KIND OF MAN
YOU WANT TO BE

The best way to predict the future is to create it.
– Abraham Lincoln

Animals follow a predetermined program. They are locked into preset behavioral commands and prompts. Some animals can be trained to mimic human ability, but this takes significant time and resources, and the scope of the outcome is incredibly limited when compared to the capabilities of even low-level humans. Animals do not have an authentic will.

But you do have an authentic will. You have creative ability that superseded your basic needs. You can imagine something and make it real, even if it wasn't real before. Look at the iPhone, the flat-screen TV, or even firearms. Humans also have this ability for themselves and their clothes. Just look at the animals we train, rags-to-riches stories, and stories of redemption. Someone had an idea about a thing or an outcome in life and they did things to make it happen.

This creative ability does not stop at your mental health, your family culture, or cycles that go from your parents to you to your kids. You have deciding power in your life. In fact, you are really the only person who truly gets to decide. No one can force on you what you have not chosen to be, do, pursue, believe, or think for yourself.

This imaginative and creative power is what we often refer to as vision. Direction is vision. Vision is the sight, foresight, and understanding of the desired outcome and reverse engineering it to where I am now so I can take actionable steps forward. Vision works for the good, the bad, the ugly, and the mediocre.

Lacking vision

Being the Man you needed + the needs of your family = direction. Working to become that man = the path forward; giving that man away = purpose. To acquire purpose, you must know what path to take, but if you do not know what direction to go you won't know which path is correct.

Without vision, you won't truly know who you are. Without the correct vision, you will be lost and end up in a place you do not belong. Dads lack vision when they have not decided who they will be for themselves but have instead allowed life and pain and their past to shape them. Lacking vision leads to chaos and foolishness, and these dads lack noble purpose and self-control.

Without a noble vision, a vision based on well-founded, virtuous, and generational blessing, the dad's vision will be corrupted by the pull of sex, money, power, popularity, or possessions. Dads corrupt their vision of themselves when they decide who they believe they are based on what best fills their hollow void.

Dads with corrupted vision use money, sex, popularity, materials, or position to attempt to fill the void of their hollow identity. Dads who lack vision fill that hollow spot with all the crap from their past and their fears about the future. Whether lacking or corrupted, these visions fail to fill the voids in the dad, and they will need to try harder to fill this void, medicating more and more with substances, laziness, comfort, or immoral behavior. They will not find the knowledge of who they are and the direction to go they have looked for, which will add agitation to their pain. Their lack of identity will drive them to find pretend fulfillment, which leaves them more unsatisfied. This increased dissatisfaction will add irritation to the pain of not knowing who they are, which will compel them to look for fulfillment outside of God, virtue, and their family, which will leave them more unsatisfied.

This is the misery loop many dads are trapped in. The dad has hurt and unmet needs from childhood or adolescence. The dad does not handle these issues in a noble way, through virtue and a clear, moral vision, but looks to the world to compensate and medicate. This teaches him escapism, pleasure-seeking, and looking for a purpose in trivial things (like money, popularity, and emotion). The man becomes a dad, which again brings up his unhealed hurts and unmet needs. He is now unable to give his wife and kids what they really need because he cannot give what he does not have, which adds more pain. He instinctively resorts to escaping, seeking pleasure, and that fake sense of purpose found in material things, but now he pursues these things even harder because his need for relief is greater because his pain is greater, because he is faced with the effects and limitations his pain has on others.

He is not at all the dad he really wants to be. As he avoids the problem, he instills escapism, pleasure-seeking, and fake purpose in his family's culture. Whether he walls up and just works to provide or pursues vices to take the edge off, he is failing to meet his family's needs. He knows this, which intensifies the cycle. He keeps looking for purpose in the same place he always loses it, and loses the trust and respect of his family at the same time. His children experience the same hurt that the dad went through, and they learn to handle it the same way they see their father handling it now. And it is always worse for the kids because, like interest, this stuff compounds over time.

This is why young girls look to the attention of perverted men, why young boys look to immoral men or even homosexuality, and why wives leave, cheat, or self-destruct. The cycle is unbroken because the hero refused to step up, and the wave kept going.

Family Second

I know because I was there. During those seven years of hell, I found such great validation in the attention and affection of people at church. I was inspiring and effective for the leaders, strangers, teammates, and the people we were serving, and this inspiration and effectiveness were not something I had at home. I garnered all sense of worth and importance and love in my position as "leader" at church because it made me feel wanted and valuable like nothing else ever had. Then, at home, I was all but unavailable to my wife and children.

Gentlemen, listen. I would talk about good character and then allow emotions to boil over on my family. I would spend hours in prayer with people but not with my wife. This went on for a few years. But it was subtle, the way an infection is at the beginning.

I was disgusted with my "family second" approach and became desperate to change. I prayed to find the man who would understand what I was going through, know how to kick my butt into gear, and would be able to teach me what I needed. "Send me someone who can help!"

The response to my prayer came in the form of two questions.

The first response was, *"What would that man be like?"*

I took the powerful principles and ideals I loved and used those to describe the kind of man who could help me. *Not afraid of his feelings. In love with his wife and kids. Sticks to the mission and his responsibilities no matter what. Keeps his chest up. Doesn't need the approval of others, but knows he is approved by God. Is a true leader, at home first and then to others. Is physically capable and dangerous. Is successful. Does not take out his pain on his family. Would know exactly what I needed to hear. Knew how to calm me down and encourage me. Would not tolerate me wallowing and would strengthen me instead of rejecting me. His faith does not waver. Shows me the way forward and walks the road with me. Not embarrassed by my struggle, but not feeling sorry for me, either. Able to teach me how to change.*

It may not seem super clear to you reading this, but God was not asking me anything. He was telling me something. The first question, *"What would that man be like?"* would provide me a glimpse of the man I was made to be. I was able to answer the question the way I did because the answer was within me. I wasn't speaking from desire but from instinctively knowing who I was made to be. Even over a decade later, I can recall the stillness and hope this exercise brought me, knowing that what I was looking for had already been built into me.

The second question: *"What is keeping you from being him?"*

It was a rhetorical question. *What will you do to be the man you need, Greg?* was the real question. Finally, after all of these years, I saw the missing piece: my path forward was to describe the man I needed and then fight like hell to be him. I did not fully understand at the time, but these two questions were the path out of the darkness that God had been trying to show me all along. Seeing the kind of man it would take to help was my direction, and the work to be like that man was the path I had to walk to get there.

I was acting like a fool, getting validation from outside sources, and causing pain in my home because I did not know who I was. Because I did not know who I was, I did not know how to live. Because I didn't know how to live, I was like a leech that latched on to anything or anyone that made me feel valuable. I had to change, but I had to know what I was changing into first, or I would repeat the same garbage.

Dads are morally obligated to squeeze vision out of their minds, using high ideals, inspiration, and noble desires to decide the kind of man they will become. If dads do not, their pain, past, and circumstances will decide for them, and it will be their children who pay the ultimate price.

APPLY THIS TODAY

Get clear on the type of man you want to be and have the courage to pursue him passionately.

This is important for all people, but especially for dads like me who were not given identity as a child. Tear off and throw out all that weak, sad crap you took on as your identity. Take your place as the hero of your bloodline.

Creating a vision like this is a critical step to winning the battle of mental health and restoring quality of life and breakthrough for our families.

1. Think about your dark moment when you were a hurt child, out of hope, ready to quit, or felt like you were drowning. Imagine a man coming in to save you, who knew exactly what to do and how to help.
   a. What is that man like?
   b. What is it about him that made him capable of saving you?
2. Who do you *NOT* want to be? In your marriage? Emotions? Thoughts? With your kids? You know what you don't want. What kind of man do you **not** want to be?
   a. Write a list of what you do not want. Ex: I do not want my wife to feel second to anyone.
   b. Flip these around to give language to what you **do** want. For example, I want my wife to know that I love her more than anyone else.
   c. Put it together as an I am statement: I am a man who loves his woman so passionately that she knows she is a priority.
3. Ask your wife and children how you have been letting them down. Yeah, this one is going to hurt but opening yourself up to this feedback is going to give you accuracy on certain changes to make at home and position you as the hero your family has been waiting for.
   a. When you ask, **do not** defend yourself. Say "thank you" and just write down what they say.
   b. How does their feedback line up with what you say you don't want? If you listed laziness and your wife said she needs you to be more reliable, BOOM.
   c. How does meeting that need line up with the man

you say you want to be?

4. Compile all of this and you have your vision. *"A man who is_____ instead of _____." "Provide_____ to my wife and children instead of _____." "When I feel/go through/ experience _____, I will do _____ instead of _____."*

a. Each answer and desire here is a single brick that will build the home of your vision.

b. Do the mental work to piece it together because this will attach your intentionality to the narrative.

DEBRIEF - DECIDE THE KIND OF MAN YOU WANT TO BE

- Dads, the direction in life that you have been looking for is combining the needs of your family with being the man that you needed as a boy.

- You have a choice in the man you become. You can choose to be someone you love, admire, and are inspired by.

- If you do not decide the kind of man you want to be, your past, your family, and society have already picked an identity for you.

- Deciding the kind of man you want to be is best done when you describe the man who could achieve and sustain what you truly want out of life.

- The bigger, the better. Make your vision as wild and fantastic as possible. Out dream your self-doubt.

XIII
RULE FIVE:
LOVE REGRET

There is no humiliation worse than the consciousness of a wasted life. It stains the spirit, forestalls hope, and destroys any motive for action or change.
– Peter Ackroyd

Remember, becoming the man you need and giving him away = purpose.

Once you determine a vision, you have a course of life that is based on noble goals, strong ideals, or service to others. Your battle goes from getting through life to filling the gap between where you are and making that vision real. When you fail to fill the gap, you have regret.

Living as a man, you do not need around = despair. Despair leads to depression and broken families. Fix the life, fix the despair. Fix the despair, fix the families.

Consider if you are proud of how you are living. I'm not

talking about comparing yourself, hating yourself, or beating yourself up. Just an honest assessment of the quality of life you are bringing to the table.

Are you living as a man that you would be proud to have around? How proud are you of your:

- Self-talk
- Effort
- Discipline
- Kindness
- Honesty
- Dedication
- Purity
- Body
- Attitude
- Success
- Relationships
- Example you set
- Marriage

These are all things you control, but forget what you control. These are the things that are affected by and a reflection of the way you are living in private. How you live in the places where only God sees you will influence everything else in life.

When we live as dads we do not respect, admire, or want to be we become half-hearted wannabes with only left-overs to give to our families. This hinders your children's development, your wife's growth, and our own mental health. So, living as a man you regret is causing you depression because you are imposing on your family and a man that you do not love.

Are you following yet?

Regret is a system, and the indicators of this system are the guilt, disappointment, or embarrassment we feel for thinking or acting like a dad who is less than the dad we said we wanted to be. Regret is not about digging through my past for crap. Nor is regret about reminding myself of all the ways I am not good enough. Regret is our internal system of feeling the pain of how I am choosing to live. Period. Regret is trying to keep me on track by helping me avoid doing the things I should not do and doing the things I know I should.

Regret is that little whisper: *Are you sure you want to do that? Why didn't you go to bed sooner? You said tomorrow, but didn't you already say that yesterday? Isn't this a waste of time? Will this get you closer to what you said you want?*

When we prolong exposure to the indicators of regret - the embarrassment, guilt, and disappointment for acting below what we said we wanted - we become depressed. Depression comes from ignoring regret the same way second-degree burns come from not taking your hand off the burner after it burned you the first time.

Regret is your best friend because regret tells you when you are drifting away from your promises or deliberately falling short of what you said you would do. When we have a clear, strong vision and we obey regret, we meet who we were made to be.

This is also why dads lack confidence: they know deep down they are full of crap because they haven't stuck to *this* or they keep going back to *that*. Dads know they can't believe themselves because they continue doing things they regret, and their self-belief is broken.

Saved On A Snowy Hill

Around 2015-2016, my self-pity was coming to a violent head. For the first time in my adult life, my depression was so bad that I didn't get out of bed for two days. My wife, Judy, attempted to spur me out of bed multiple times because, for two days, I broke a promise to my daughter. My daughter was four and I promised to take her sledding. For the last two days, we were hammered with snow, and sledding conditions were perfect. Amara got in and out of her snow gear multiple times as my wife made excuses for me. On the third day, Judy had enough.

She came into our room and closed the door behind her, forcing herself to speak with anger. "You promised your daughter that you would take her sledding, and the snow will be gone tomorrow. She has waited two days. Do not be the dad who breaks his promise. Get up and be a man."

So I did. I put Amara in the car, hit Target to buy a new sled, and went to the biggest hill in our area.

We were on the cold, snowy hill for hours. Amara had icicles in her hair, but we both had enough energy to keep going. Eventually, she wanted to go down by herself. I asked if she was aware she could get hurt, and she said she wanted to go down anyway. So I put her in the sled and sent her flying!

As I watched her fly down the hill, time slowed and almost stood still. I saw how happy my child was and how I had tried to take that away from her by feeling sorry for myself. I saw my life on a linear scale and recalled every person whose life had forever changed because of how I showed up for them. I saw myself as the people who loved me saw me - important, capable, valued - and then I saw myself as I felt I was - broken, small, weak.

Then, there was a question that gripped my mind: *If the way you felt about yourself was written on your tombstone, would you be proud?*

My problem was not that I didn't know who I was or that I was unaware of what I was capable of. I knew who I was. I remembered Nathan's dream and the vision from when I was 16 every day. My problem was that I allowed thoughts in my mind that did not line up with who I knew I was. My problem was that I allowed my feelings to alter my expectations, change the story I was telling to myself, and, most importantly, influence how I behaved day to day.

It was not loud or overwhelming, but I suddenly felt the weight of how much time and energy I wasted wallowing. Guilt engulfed my heart because, for years, I had focused on my feelings and taken away from the people I loved. My heart broke because I finally saw how what I had been going through was not the real pain I had suffered. My lack of physical and mental fortitude was.

This experience gave me one of the most important lessons of my life: it wasn't what was happening that made me so depressed I could barely move. I was depressed because I used my feelings as an excuse to break my promises. How embarrassing to have experienced such incredible things and still choose self-pity!

I had literally saved lives, traveled the world, and built a local reputation for helping the helpless, fed and clothed 1,000s of homeless men and women, bringing many to faith in Christ. I helped young men let go of the fear of failure and pursue their dreams. I had been a father to the fatherless. I came from a horrible place and won the heart of a saintly woman. I was a pillar of faith and strength in our community.

Was I really about to give it all up for bad feelings? I was really going to forget everything I had done up to that point because of what I was struggling with? How could I possibly believe I was worthless and ineffective with this list of accomplishments? I had accomplished more in a few years than many others accomplished in their lifetime. Losers don't do what I have done, which meant I was not a loser.

Dads, as I took in the regret of thinking and acting like such a fool, I was filled with pride and gratitude. Hard truths have always given me peace. Facing the pain of my regrets gave me clarity, and with that clarity, I found the strength to get up and act like the man I knew I wanted to be. The storm broke at that moment. No joke. That's all it took - facing the pain, listening to regret, and being the best for my daughter in the moment.

For two days, I did not get out of bed because of what I felt. If I had embraced Amara and focused on her above what I was feeling, I would have been better. In that moment on the hill I had a sense of direction, understanding, and purpose. I found them face-to-face with life, not in my prayers, while I stayed in bed and waited for God to rescue me. Truth is, I hated that version of Greg, the one that was so weak against what he was going through. He looked nothing like the heroes I had, the man I wanted to be, or the man I promised to my wife and kids.

Was I still battling severe mental and emotional issues? Are dads lacking guidance through complex problems? Are we dealing with wounds from a broken home? Sure, but the path forward finally made sense. The better I got at being good at being a man, the better I would be as a husband and father. The better I was as a husband and father, the better their lives would be. And then how hard would it be to believe I was lost and hopeless? I had to amass evidence of the goodness my actions created for you at home, and it would force the storm to acquiesce.

Regret & Depression

I turned listening to regret into a skill and started teaching it to others. Regret is critical in us becoming the dads our children will love following.

I had already listed the man I wanted to be in my vision. Laying in bed feeling sorry for himself wasn't on the list. Allowing depression to keep me from taking my daughter sledding wasn't on the list. Being lazy, scared, and passive because I was struggling was NOT ON THE LIST.

Do you know what *was* on the list? ***Living a life of courage not comfort; not letting my problems boil over in the home; controlling my emotions; staying ahead of the storm by living right.*** My depression got worse because I, in the moment, decided to compromise on the man I said I wanted to be, prioritizing my own feelings over keeping my promise to my daughter.

Let's be real: the sledding story is a dramatic realization, but there were a million other little regrets. Being snippy because I was tired because I stayed up too late. Feeling bad about myself because I listened to my fear and missed an opportunity. Not going for that run I felt compelled to go on and feeling down because I didn't feel confident. Not shutting my phone off to be with my kids instead of being entertained.

This is why staying in regret leads to depression. When you do things that you know you should not be doing, you carry the shame of it, whether you want to admit the shame or not.

Men are designed to be creatively powerful, dependable, and honorable. There is no honor in breaking the promises we make to ourselves and others. I am not dependable if I ignore what I ought to do so I can do the thing I feel like doing. I have no power to bear the weight of my life and family if I cannot even bear the weight of my momentary plight or desire.

Again, as the theme continues, it is not what happened to us that did the most harm but how we allowed it to shape our beliefs and actions.

In every part of your life where your actions don't match what you say you believe, you are lowering yourself into depression. In every way you work to make all parts of your life match the vision, you are elevating yourself into the quality of life, breakthrough, and peace.

————

APPLY THIS TODAY

People who avoid feeling regret are rejecting a superhuman ability. When you have your mind set on doing the right thing, and you are working to make your life count for someone else, listening to regret is a super power because it shields you against doubt and shame at the same time as it shows God that you are trustworthy to receive what He has for you.

Eliminating regret makes you feel better and builds your confidence. You feel better for doing the right thing, even if you didn't want to. Your confidence grows because you proved to yourself that you are a man of your word. Confidence unlocked!

You can do more than just correct regrettable actions. By listening to regret, you can train your mind to think forward, and avoid regrettable things altogether. .

1. First, get real about what you are doing that you regret.
   a. What would you be embarrassed to let other people know?
   b. What behaviors are you justifying or making excuses for?
      i. *"I smoke pot cuz _____."*
      ii. *"I haven't worked out cuz _____."*
      iii. *"I would be closer to my kids, but _____."*
   c. Write a list of all those things you know you need to get to work on. Do not make it just big things, like "workout" or "start a business." Make it clear: go for a run this afternoon, have that conversation, and turn the TV off.
      i. Start: what things do you know you need to start?
         1. Includes learning or pursuing dreams.
      ii. Stop: what things do you know you need to stop?
         2. Includes people you hang with.
2. Make a list of what supports or hinders what you say you want:
   a. Take the narrative of the man you want to be and write down where the gaps are between you and him. Write down answers to each. Next to each answer,

write either "supports" or "hinders." The "hinder" actions are those that need to be replaced by more supporting actions. The supporting actions are those you need to double down on. I have added examples from my own life below to help guide you.

i. What habits do you have?
    1. The habit of working out = supports
    2. Staying up late watching movies = hinders
ii. What thoughts are you thinking?
    1. The call on my life and how to make it real = supports
    2. What a loser I am for having a hard time = hinders
iii. What friendships do you have?
    1. Guys from the trailer park who still get high and party = hinders
    2. Business owners and pastors who have good marriages and strong bodies = supports
iv. What content are you consuming?
    1. Mostly meaningless videos on YouTube = hinders
    2. Podcasts on mindset and books on stoicism = supports
v. How are you handling hardship, confrontation, and your past?
    1. Forgiveness = supports
    2. Feeling like a failure every time something goes wrong = hinders.

- Dad, becoming the man you needed and giving him away is your purpose.

- Living a life you regret is a commitment to poor mental health and a low quality of life.

- If you learn to love and listen to regret, you will save yourself years of pain and failure.

- The majority of what people would describe as depression is actually regret: the regret of allowing their pleasure and emotions to dictate their thoughts and behaviors; the guilt of not keeping their word to themselves; the embarrassment of saying they want something and not really putting up the effort to get it.

- Scrutinize which thoughts and actions support or hinder what you say you want and believe, and turn this into a skill.

XIV
RULE SIX:
DEVELOP YOURSELF INTO A MAN

Desiring their freedom, He therefore refuses to carry them,
by their mere affections and habits, to any of the goals which
He sets before them: He leaves them to 'do it on their own.'
— C.S. Lewis, The Screwtape Letters

Dads, fatherhood is a high-demand job. We often feel stressed, exhausted, or overwhelmed with the added burden being a dad puts on our lives. A lot of dads secretly regret having kids and feel terrible for feeling that way. Some dads hate themselves because they can only see how they are failing or inadequate. Fatherhood puts on us a demand that we are just not ready for. Even dads from amazing families aren't ready, so if you came from a broken home like I did, no duh, you are stressed.

Fatherhood will demand more of you than you are able to give, and that is because you must change to be the dad your kids need. How many dads weren't shown how to be present, loving fathers because they didn't have a present, loving father as a boy? You don't know how to give what your kids need because you didn't receive it for yourself. You are stressed and exhausted because these demands are pulling from that proverbially empty cup. Yes, you have work to do, and yes, you need to change, but show yourself some mercy here, brother.

And listen - THIS IS NOT A DEATH SENTENCE. It is easily overcome. You can give away what you never received when you become something you've never been. That is what this entire book, and this chapter particularly, is about. Being what you have not been to have what you have not had.

This chapter will inspire and teach you how to generate the power, clarity, and stillness in private that fills you up so you are not drained by the demands of your life. This is how I have been able to create for my kids an amazing world I had zero paradigm for. I built something for my kids that I had never even seen, and I will show you how to as well.

Good is not good enough

I was good at being a good man, but I was terrible at being good at being a man. I was polite but not strong, nice but not disciplined, passionate but not tested. It wasn't that God made me depressed to punish me, but God used this pain to build in me the virtue and character that I allowed my pain to tarnish.

Earlier, I stated multiple times that what I chose was more

harmful to me than anything else. My greatest pain, beyond the abuse and the suicide and the mental health problems, was how much I shrunk back based on my pain. I shrank back, and it was from that small, craven place where I lived for a long time. During that time, I learned patterns of thought and behavior, responding this way to that thing or that way to this one. I trained myself to shrink my potential, my esteem, my abilities, and my faith. That is where my depression was coming from.

What I needed was not more sympathy, more understanding, or more trying. I was hurting myself by shrinking back, so I had to grow forward as a man to change my situation.

Self-development was the missing piece that, once I had it, set everything else in order. The reason why self-development was *the* game changer for me is the exact reason why regret is so important:

> *Remember, it is sin to know what you ought*
> *to do and then not do it.*
> *– James 4:17*

The mind, time, and body are designed to function in a certain way in conjunction with virtue. Throughout human history, people from every culture have understood that the pursuit of virtuous conduct - self-control, discipline, justice, service, etc.—is man's moral obligation, and when these virtues are lacking, people, families, and society suffer.

We know we must also do what is right with our bodies, our

time, and our minds. This is why righteousness and prosperity are contrasted against laziness, foolishness, and selfishness. Improper use of the mind leads to foolishness, doubt, and fear, while proper use of the mind leads to wisdom, faith, and intellect. Improper use of the body leads to sexual immorality, compromise, and overindulgence, while proper use of the body leads to capability, recognition, and self-control (which is a fruit of the Spirit for believers who might try refuting this). Improper use of time leads to laziness, wasted life, and offering little value, while proper use of our time leads to value, productivity, and success.

This is what I was getting wrong the entire time.

Doing the right thing is so much more than just morality; it is also about function. Morally, I was solid and immovable, but I just kept running in circles with my drive to do the right moral thing. Functionally, I was disobedient, wayward, and flippant. I just didn't know, and as much as the leaders in my life loved me, they didn't know, either.

I have said many times the one true cure for depression is to get so damn good at being a dad you admire that you see the benefits it has for your family, and the darkness will melt away. Self-development is the *how* of getting that damn good.

When I started keeping promises to myself, my self-respect increased, and my shame decreased. When I respected myself more, I was more capable, and my sex drive increased, which made my wife more attracted to me and more sexually satisfied. When I got in better shape, my edginess wore off, and my family stopped walking on eggshells at home. When I truly cared more about my family than anyone else and refused to receive validation from those people, we were happier and closer!

When I added self-development to the work I was doing and the character I already had, things got so much better at home for my wife and kids that our quality of life exploded, and the darkness fell off. The nasty thoughts in my head were mockable now because I was proud of myself for living like a badass. How could I feel insecure about other people's thoughts when my own family honestly admired me? How could I have doubt about myself when I could look at how far I had already come and see that I was only getting better, not slowing down or backing off?

I utilized my mind, body, and time to improve and felt whole, powerful, steady, and proud. Those traumatic episodes lessened from months to weeks and from weeks to minutes. I had finally figured out how to win: moment to moment.

What I Was Missing

I was a good Christian. I obeyed the text, thought the right thoughts and did the right things, but not consistently and not with the right priorities. I knew the truth and how to use it, but would wallow for hours. I would set suffering aside to serve my church but struggled to do this at home.

I leaned on my spiritual knowledge and hope more than I leaned on the intellect God gave me. I was waiting for Him to make it happen while He was waiting for me to figure it out.

I leaned on His promise to provide more than I leaned on my creative power and abilities. I was waiting for the good stuff to crash through the walls, and He was waiting for me to develop my abilities and go into the world and do something with them.

It wasn't about the calling. It wasn't about the past in any shape or form.

What I was missing was the character it would take to achieve and sustain transformation at a family level and the expertise to help dads do the same, in that order.

Jesus was not a bag of milk

When you recall William Wallace fighting to liberate Scotland, do you imagine him as a scrawny nerd who had never worked out a day in his life?

When you hear of George Washington riding through volleys of musket fire and demanding the courage of his men, does George look fat or fit?

When the Bible says Jesus is returning soaked in the blood of His enemies, do you imagine Jesus' man boobs bouncing up and down in sync with the gallops of His horse?

How would John Wick's story have ended if he was so out of shape he could barely climb stairs?

Imagine Aragorn, Christian from Pilgrim's Progress, or even

Katniss Everdeen with muffin tops spilling out of their armor, sweaty double chins, unable to run, or so weak they couldn't do a single push-up!

The stories would have been completely different.

God could trust David to slay Goliath because David *already* killed a lion and a bear. He was selected because he was *already* strong, brave, and full of faith. Yet we are waiting to be strong and brave and full of faith until we are called, which is why we haven't been called.

We have a society of families led by men who look like they have breasts, are too embarrassed to take their shirts off, and are not physically capable of working, moving, or fighting.

God designed us to respond to appearance a certain way because we all understand what a person's appearance says about their priorities, mindset, and private life.

There is one type of physical appearance that communicates instant gratification, lack of commitment, and comfort.

There is another physical appearance that communicates hard work, commitment, and capability.

Do not take this in any form as me saying we need a 6-pack to be saved or righteous. Not at all, but we need to stop pretending that how we treat our bodies is insignificant. There is a real problem with how men are living in private, and it is our families and communities that are suffering because of it.

Self-excellence Is Honor

The Glory of God is man fully alive.
– Attributed to St. Irenaeus

Self-excellence is one of the greatest forms of honor and gratitude.

Self-excellence is the use of my mind, body, and time for self-mastery and the achievement of high ideals. To devote my life to being capable of giving the utmost is to live by honor, and capability is the fruit of self-excellence. Striving to improve in all the areas that make me, me is to display my gratitude for what I have in life. Passions. Talents and abilities. Physical fitness and health. Mental acuity. Masculinity. The more developed I am in each area, the better I can serve people, the more confident I will be, and the stronger sense of value I will have in life.

How can I better show my value than:

- Using the willpower to control my thoughts and direct them in a way that makes life better...

- Developing my body so I am able to move, work, and protect the helpless for long periods of time without reasonable accommodation...

- Eliminating waste from how I spend my time to the point that when I set a goal, it gets achieved, and when I am assigned a task, it gets completed...

To live a mediocre life of pleasure and comfort demands nothing great of you. Can you still be good? Can you still make money? Are you still loved? Of course, but when did we get so small that we are happy doing the bare minimum?

Those in history who tore down empires, slayed giants, broke oppression, and won wars did not do so from the comfort of their leisure and desires but in the heat of strife after having first overcome their own weaknesses and excuses.

Fatherhood is about mitigating the negative and instilling the great, living in such a way as to impact a future he will never see by the example he sets.

How in the hell do you expect to do this full of excuses, indulgence, and fear?

APPLY THIS TODAY

Every hero, including Jesus, had to grow in favor with God and with man. Because they grew in these areas, they were trusted with greater things which allowed them to do more and more for God and others.

4 Pillars of self-development:

1. **Think & Study Like A Hero:** Daily Intellectual Growth.
   a. Maintain control of your mind.
      i. Do daily mind work exercises.
      ii. Live with valor inside your own head.

b. Read stoicism.

c. Get a guide.

    i. You need a positive male role model (father figure, coach, etc.)

    ii. Violently pursue and apply wise counsel.

d. Filter every thought, experience, emotion, and course of action through high ideals and a standard of truth.

e. Increase decisiveness.

    i. No more winging it. Have a plan and stick to it.

    ii. I don't care, "What do you want to eat/watch/do?"

2. **Train & Look Like A Hero:** Daily Physical Growth

a. Be skilled.

    i. Identify your abilities and practice them.

    ii. Be capable of different things so you can be more useful in general.

b. Look like a man.

    i. Get fit and lose the fat. Stop eating junk foods, stop eating until you are full, do four high-intensity workouts each week, and drink a gallon of water per day.

    ii. Stand up straight and make eye contact.

    iii. Dress like you are someone you care about.

c. Practice self-defense.

    i. Spar.

    ii. Shoot.

    iii. Pay attention to your surroundings.

d. Keep routines. Morning, evening, prayer, etc. This instills discipline.

    i. Maintain good hygiene first thing each morning.

    ii. Be up before you need to and stay up no later than is necessary.

    iii. Generate focus and power before the demands of life hit you so that you can give with a full cup.

  e. Work daily to display justice, integrity, discipline, courage, and compassion.

3. **Believe & Sacrifice Like A Hero:** Daily Spiritual Growth

  a. Stubbornly optimistic.

    i. Zero tolerance for doubt and fear.

    ii. Talk about how God previously solved a similar problem and ask Him to do it again now.

  b. Develop moral fortitude.

    i. Pursue what is right above anything else.

    ii. Cut immorality and vice from your life.

    iii. No pretending, lying, or excuses.

  c. Be vulnerable with your moral standards.

    i. Judge yourself ruthlessly each day on your moral conduct.

  d. Study the word of God and pray.

  e. Make forgiveness a priority.

4. **Find A Team & Serve Like A Hero:** Daily Character Growth

  a. Find groups of like-minded men to be part of. Brotherhood is key.

    i. Let good men judge you.

    ii. Help other men and allow them to help you.

  b. Do not be the one to cause division or problems.

    i. Avoid gossip. Have hard talks with the correct people. Forgive and let go of mistakes.

ii. Don't treat people differently because of their beliefs but because of their character.

c. Keep the promises you make to yourself.

i. Do in private what you want to be known for in public.

d. Impose goodness on your environment.

i. Hold doors.

ii. Push cars that are stuck.

iii. Clean up after yourself, even at a restaurant.

iv. Wipe up that piss and facial hair. Never allow your women to use a dirty toilet or sink.

e. Burden yourself with serving others.

i. First in the home.

ii. How can you be more reliable, available, and beneficial to someone else?

DEBRIEF - SELF-DEVELOPMENT

- Dads, your path through depression, despair, and dissatisfaction is the process of becoming the kind of man who can achieve and sustain love and closeness with your family.

- You are the hero in your story, but you are also the guide to their story. Act like it.

- Boil your life down to the moment and the day. Be here now. Not back that way. Not up there.

- Create a habit of scrutinizing your daily effort - mentally, emotionally, and physically. *What am I proud of from today (self-gratitude and giving self credit)? What doubts or dark things did I let in today? How might I have wallowed?*

- This is not about you making yourself good enough. You are already irreplaceable as a son. This is about you becoming more so you can give more.

XV
RULE SEVEN:
EFT

Those who despair at every setback do not have the strength to carry the more.
– Loren Sandford

"Get back up. Every. F***ing. Time." Nathan Sandford, my first pastor, taught me EFT. When I was struggling to break away from my friends, stay sober, and truly commit to the Lord in that first year, EFT was the expectation. This was profound for us young men who came from homes where we were terrified of making mistakes, convinced we would fail, or anxiously driven to be perfect.

EFT means turning my pain into aggression. It is about using the pain of my struggles to push me into change. It is about not allowing the pity of my struggles to cause me to quit but motivating me to keep going. This is the art of falling down seven times and getting back up eight.

EFT is about resisting shame and self-criticism. It became the skill of separating the knowledge that I screwed up from what I believed about myself and the choices I made moving forward. It takes faith and strength to know that I messed up and still not allow shame or fear to run through my mind.

EFT was the fuel we used to receive discipline, learn from our mistakes, and not get caught in the sticky web of talking myself out of big dreams because of *this failure* or *that issue*. This was our name for a growth mindset.

EFT was a disdain we had for acquiescence, quitting, and mediocrity.

When you are scared, hurting, and even alone.

EFT.

When you want to quit, cannot see the point of hope, or want to tell yourself the lie that you've done everything you should, and it's just not working.

EFT.

When you fail, hurt someone you love, or can't seem to get it right.

EFT.

This was to truly not quit. To fall and stay down was fear, pride, or avoidance. There is no courage or faith in giving up. Think of how often we give up in little ways - the promises about tomorrow, "I guess one won't hurt," "I need to lighten up a little," - and we wonder why men lack purpose and feel empty.

This was also how we learned humility, though none of us really knew it at the time: to get wounded or stumble and return to the frey voluntarily. To get back up, especially in those early days, was humiliating, but we faced it. I had to live from a place of perseverance even when I thought I was not worthy, when I didn't think I had what it would take, when I thought other people were so much more qualified than I was. EFT meant I could no longer hide in shame. No matter how badly I felt or screwed up, I had to force my heart and mind to stay open to receiving God's love, listening to my brothers at church, and keeping the promises I made. Resisting our desire to hide or protect ourselves emotionally actually protected us. It taught us how to fall forward and kept us from sliding into relapse if we slipped.

Lastly, and more importantly, to me, EFT was duty. I could not quit just because I had a bad day or made a bad call. EFT was not just enduring tough times but changing into the man I needed to be to accomplish my mission *despite* the tough times. People were counting on me as an example and a guide, so EFT was just the right thing to do.

Dog Soldiers & Their Dog Rope

Cheyenne Dog Soldiers were known for their bravery and aggression, their skill in battle, and their willingness to die before retreating. Like many Native warriors, they were fierce and they were feared. What sets Dog Soldiers apart from others, though, is the reason for the name: the Dog Rope.

The Dog Rope was an 8' to 12' long strip of rawhide, attached at one end to a stake and to the Dog Soldier at the other. This stake would be driven into the ground during battle, and the attached Dog Soldier could not move beyond the length of his tether. Retreat was impossible.

In fact, the Dog Soldier was not allowed to remove his stake from the ground by himself. Another party member could remove the stake if they deemed the Dog Soldier performed with valor and honor. The use of a Dog Rope in battle was comparable to a suicide mission.

When a Dog Soldier staked his Dog Rope into the ground, he did not plan on leaving the battlefield but fighting to the death.

EFT is your Cookie-Cutter

You see, it wasn't the mantra EFT by itself that kept us going. EFT was my Dog Rope, and my battlefield was the idea I held on to. I had tethered myself to an idea that if I lived my life well, I could impact eternity for someone else. That required a way of life, a set of values, and a stubborn persistence to endure. Because I tethered myself to an outcome bigger than myself, I was able to truly change.

This is also exactly why so many men find change somewhat impossible: they are tethered to something that is not what they say they want. They want respect but are tethered to comfort. They want purpose but are tethered to pleasure or position or money. They cannot get far from screwing up because their heart is not set on the noble outcome they say they want.

Your Dog Rope is your true desire and will be a cookie-cutter in your life, cutting away everything that doesn't fit your desires. My Dog Rope was the vision I had and the hope to impact others, which forced me to be shaped by noble pursuits and service. Other men's Dog Rope is their pleasure and the drive to have their way no matter what, forcing them into a life of indulgence. My Dog Rope forced me to change, to get better as a man, to withstand hardship, and prove to myself I was capable of my mission. Other dads have a Dog Rope that forces them to keep drinking, to stay fat or lazy, or to stay checked out despite the evident pain it is causing their family and themselves.

I refused to move from executing on my mission and other dads refused to move from their comfort, pleasure, and excuses.

From the night I woke up after attempting suicide up to today, we have experienced drastic and common struggles. The 7-year psychosis, during which I was in a critical state, batting suicide and what seemed like endless depression. During my time in the church mentoring youth, we lost multiple kids to suicide, had others attempt it, lost kids to drugs, alcohol, and crime, and had one youth get caught up in a murder case. I got married and had two kids (both events are known to be stress-inducing). Friends and family went through divorces. Death and loss in our personal relationships. Issues in the church caused division.

And still, at the end of the day, I kept my Dog Rope firmly embedded in my vision and my promises.

Someone will say, "Yeah, but that's life. We all go through things."

Yup, but there is a reason I have survived insane things and am still a better dad than many..

I have been through more than most people and have had a better life than most people. That is why I wrote this book: what I have is not unique to me. I am not better than any other dad; I just made different choices and made a powerful life, and am trying to help dads do the same.

Staying Down: EFT

You are either getting back up or you are not. To stay down is to make your struggle greater than the needs of those around you and the promise you made.

Staying down breeds selfishness, and it happens when we medicate, isolate, or salivate:

- Medicate: the use of anything to numb or escape the sensation of the current situation without having fully faced or worked through it. Anything you give your body, time, or mind to in order to lessen the pain.

Something you prioritize over handling the situation (I can't do this because ___) *or* use to get out of it without resolving it (Needed this ____ because I was having a terrible day). This can be nicotine, food, sex, recognition, porn, alcohol, drugs, prayer, compliments, doing nice things for others, work, video games, exercise, creating content, masturbation, chores, taking care of the kids, hobbies, yard work, errands, talking with a mentor or therapist, etc. Literally, anything that allows you to avoid the problem so you can feel better. This makes you selfish because you make yourself incapable of handling the stress or pain, and you end up addicted to the escape instead of the process of overcoming.

· A Dog Soldier does not abandon his place to run and feel better.

- Isolate: Not reaching out to your people. Keeping secrets. Saying, "Yeah, no, we're great," every time someone asks. Not allowing others to know what you are going through or doing. Staying by yourself.

  · A Dog Soldier does not allow his humiliation or insecurities as an excuse to hide.

- Salivate: consumed with want. "I want to get better." "I want to change." "I hate how I am." Statistically, you actually probably don't want to change or hate where you are. A lot of people are full of regret and remorse for their predicament, but if they can find a way to feel better and stay the same, they will. They don't really hate where they are; they just hate that they got caught and are feeling the consequences.

· A Dog Soldier does not prioritize his preference or desire over the mission.

APPLY THIS TODAY

Ultimately, EFT is a line drawn in the sand. Either to change or stay the same.

EFT is a rule to never quit the good fight. What are you willing to give up, go through, or become to bring the change your family needs?

OR...

EFT is a rule to never truly let go of having your cake and eating it, too. What are you willing to give up, go through, and become to keep your pleasures and comforts and avoid the pain of radical change?

1. What idea are you tethered to?
   a. What are your habits and constant battles? Mistakes or stupid behaviors you keep repeating? This is what you are tying your Dog Rope to.
   b. What is your typical response when the pain comes on?
   c. How can you embrace this idea of EFT?
2. What recent mistakes have you made that caused you to

hide, quit, or isolate?

3. Pick a recent failure, mistake, or screw-up. How can you apply EFT? What does getting back up look like? What do you do once you are up?

4. Let go of shame. EFT applies to you being irreplaceable as a son, so hold onto it. You are not expected to be perfect, so allow rule 2 to be strong in your heart and mind even when you fall.

DEBRIEF - EVERY F***ING TIME

- We must protect ourselves from the slippery slope of giving up when we struggle. Many struggles we face on our journey are not permanent failures or mortal sins, but we incriminate and punish ourselves all the same. This is corrosive.

- Your commitments are cookie-cutter and will continue to shape your life until you become a perfect vessel for what you desire and are determined to get.

- Stop slowing down, giving up, doubting, or questioning at every little hiccup or disturbance. Push through, man.

- Evaluate your plan and assess key indicators like performance or value, but do not ever give up.

XVI

RULE EIGHT:
CARRY A NOBLE BURDEN

**This is the cost of living. For you to be here with us and do
what God has called you to do means you have to endure
this. This is the price you have to pay to be here.**
– Judy Wanberg (my wife)

"Suffering builds character" is one of the stupidest things I've
ever heard. I know good men suffering doubt and fear and
the guilt of letting their dreams die. I suffered plenty before
Christ and even after Christ because of my own flaws and
failures. Suffering is no more a merit than having lungs.

The idea that suffering builds character is the participation
trophy of trauma. Wah. Life is supposed to reward you with
strong virtue just because you had a hard time? Hell no.

Everyone suffers, but is everyone more patient? More loving?
More honest? More courageous? No, no, no, and no. Suffering
by itself isn't even what makes people selfish, weak, or timid,
either. A great human flaw is that we care little about how our

moment-to-moment attitudes, beliefs, and choices actually shape us.

It is not *that* you suffer but *how* you suffer that changes you. We don't need less suffering; we need to suffer more well so we can win and achieve more.

You are going to suffer anyway; you might as well turn the story into one in which you are the hero enduring rigorous training that will help you terrify your enemies, save the princess, and lead your kingdom into prosperity and abundance.

This is not about you.

This isn't happening to you. The heartache, the delay, the letdown, the strain of overcoming gaps in your past as you try to be the man they need at the same time. Depression is not some affliction upon you because of the failure of your parents or leaders or whatever.

Some say that *this* isn't happening to you; it is happening for you. I do not believe that is true, either.

This is happening *so that you* can be the one to break this cycle so your children are more free, more blessed, and more moral. Period. *You* are experiencing these struggles, so *you* can take up your kingly authority to raise your children in the victory of the battles you won so they can maintain and expand it.

You don't have to. You get to.

___

Until and unless you begin viewing all of your troubles as 1). the gift that will prepare you for your mission and 2). an opportunity to block these issues from passing on to your kids, you will miss out on the real growth, real change, and real impact that you were made for.

The process of enduring, thinking right, acting right, and developing yourself in the midst of these dark storms is training you. This is your "hero's training" montage in real-time. You are being prepared for something bigger and earning the authority that will allow you to help others overcome, too.

Face the struggle, acknowledge the training it provides, and embrace the benefit it will have for your children. Struggle + (training x benefit) = purpose.

Example: Struggling with addiction means you are the one to break the addiction, so your children are free from it.

Struggling with self-doubt means you get to increase confidence and hope in your kids.

Struggling with money = about your kids' wealth.

Struggling with hope = about your kids' optimism.

Struggling with mediocrity = about your kids having the best damn lives possible.

This is not about you. Embrace this, brother. It's okay.

The Stretch

Nathan taught me about the pain of living between two conflicting realities. In one reality, I know where I am, where I've been, what I've done, and the limitations I am faced with. In the other reality I know exactly who I am made to be.

You will either experience the passive pain of knowing two realities exist but never breaking out of the 1st, *or* you will experience the purposeful pain of crawling toward the second reality and making the necessary sacrifices along the way.

Purposeful pain is the heart-wrenching pause once you realize that, as beautiful and true as your vision might be, the work to achieve it is damn near impossible. It will take more of you than you have to give. It is the gut-twisting awareness that, though the man you've decided to be is real in you already, you must become a different man entirely. Once the excitement of hope and inspiration fade and you are left with the knowledge of where you are and the knowledge of who you could be, you understand how massive the task at hand truly is and your heart sinks because of it.

This is the stretch: to have more required of you than who you are is capable of delivering.

To continue reaching for a reality so far beyond where you currently are that you may not make it, but to reach anyway and not flinch. That is stretchiness. Men are judged on their stretchiness. This is the reality of what people mean when they say "effort over perfection."

The work of figuring out how to live like the man you need is like the growth that comes from reaching for a higher standard. Identity is something we were given before birth, but it is something we become through the labor of figuring it out. It has been in you since before birth, but it is your pursuit of and obedience to the vision of that man that brings him to life.

The stretch is your noble burden. To feel the pain of the ambition and effort to be of great value to others. To despise the selfish pursuit of merely feeling better. To decide that this pattern ends with you and that you are going to become the man who can create in his home the life he wasn't given.

Brother, you are going to be in pain regardless. You might as well do something awesome with it.

Stop raising children

There is a wildly popular quote by G. Michael Hopf floating around to illustrate the reason behind much of the societal turmoil we see today. *"Hard times create strong men, strong men create good times, good times create weak men, and weak men create hard times."*

It sounds good on paper but demands nothing great of us. This mindset is passive, hopeless, and negligent. Though undoubtedly powerful and commanding of attention, I personally detest this quote. It implies that men are trapped in an endless cycle of fighting for justice and prosperity, only to see their efforts undermine future generations through moral compromise and weakness borne from the very prosperity they fought for.

To acquiesce to forces outside of our control is passivity. To believe that our efforts are futile is hopelessness. To depend on external forces for the health of our family is negligence. Passive men lack purpose because only action breeds value. Hopeless men lack peace because without hope there is no security and without security there can be no peace. Negligent men lack confidence because they know their inaction makes them full of crap. Lacking confidence, internal unrest, and feeling like life has no meaning are all related to depression.

Do you really want to believe that every good thing you do will lead to unnecessary suffering because your goodness makes your children weak?

What the hell are we teaching here?

I refuse to believe that we only either fight through hard times or are spoiled by good times. I believe we can do both, and am convinced that the primary function of every man is to do exactly that: to fight and endure, and also educate their children on the past and make them capable of carrying the torch forward. Our job is to raise warriors, not just to fight wars and let the consequences unfold as they may.

Good and bad times ebb and flow. I believe we're responsible for raising our sons and daughters into men and women of such strong virtue that they impose their will on the world and shape it.

Fathers have a duty to lead their children into hardship **and** abundance. This is our burden:

- To love our children so much that, no matter what life throws at them, they know who they are and where home is. If they do not always know where home is, I failed.

- To be hard enough on them, they know no matter what happens, they are responsible and have what it takes. If they are unprepared, I fail.

These nine rules make us the kind of men who raise leaders, not children. By exemplifying the nine rules laid out in this book, we will educate our children as we grow, and our children will willingly carry the mission on their own shoulders because we have won their hearts.

Then, our children will be the strong ones who create and protect the good times and create good times even from the bad ones.

Do not abandon your post.

We are the pathfinders, guiding our people to the right future. We are the watchmen in the towers, looking over the city as they go about their lives. This is in our design.

Duty is refusing to let your pain keep you from using your gifts, abilities, or presence to bless others.

To find the challenge in your pain that will help you grow and change. What insecurity, flaw, or weakness is this exposing in me?

To not fail those who will benefit from what you learn along the way. What is this situation potentially taking away from someone else?

A worthy burden is turning your pain into a helpful lesson for someone else.

A worthy burden is identifying the threats to abundance, love, and hope in your mind and getting the help and tools to eradicate them.

A worthy burden is deciding that you are going to be responsible for doing the work to make sure none of your pain pushes on to your kids instead of being responsible for their issues in life.

A worthy burden is the sacrifice, effort, work, and growth required to be more as a dad so I can *give* more as a dad.

The cost of living

You're either having a hard time because of what you are suffering with, or you are having a hard time because you are fighting back and holding onto the faith in the midst of it.

It's hard to feel what you're feeling, and it's hard to not let those feelings shape your behavior.

There is pain and trying to figure out life the hard way because no one showed you, and there is pain and getting back up every time because you said you would, even though you don't want to.

Pain is guaranteed. You will either suffer the pain of what happened to you or you will suffer the pain of doing the work necessary in order to keep what happened to you from harming your loved ones.

APPLY THIS TODAY

1. Start seeing your actions as 90-year ripples. How you live today will impact people in 90 years. So then, what quality of life will your great-grandchildren have?
2. Change the story you are telling yourself:
   a. Not seeing what I know is true = my faith is getting stronger.
   b. Struggling to believe and stay positive = this is killing my shallow focus.
   c. Feeling down on myself = killing my selfishness.
3. Involve your kids.
   a. Tell them your story (without the crude details).
      i. Let them know why you sometimes struggle (without using them to validate yourself).
      ii. Talk with them about legacy and the future of the family (without making them responsible for you feeling accepted or successful).
4. Stop getting high. Stop drinking. Stop looking at porn. Stop losing your temper and making excuses. Get up.

Simmer in your pain without running from it as you work through it like a man.

DEBRIEF - A NOBLE BURDEN

- Dads, life is going to be hard, and you will endure pain. You can either endure the pain of your own stupidity and indulgence or the pain of becoming more so you can give more to others.

- If the primary focus of your pursuits is your feelings or your personal benefit, you will shape yourself into a hollow man.

- Carrying a noble burden is our duty because it empowers us to truly invest in and impact those who look to us.

- Let go of your reactionary need to medicate the pain. Face it and feel it so you can heal from it.

- The struggles you face in life are yours to break for your children, and that can only happen if you face them head-on and do the work to change them.

XVII
RULE NINE:
WIN THEIR HEARTS

Win his heart, Greg, and he will follow you.
– Penny Leon

"I hate not being closer to my kids." "I hate how I keep hurting them." "I hate how distant my wife and I are."

Until and unless we are actually winning their hearts and living as legacy-minded leaders, we are lying to say we hate the way things are. If we are not making active, violent changes to our lives, we don't hate what is happening, only how it feels.

Prove your hate.

Prove how much you hate it by desecrating it. If you truly hate it, you will change.

Trust me. I was so desperate to change that I would lose my voice, praying for it. And still, I made my wife's life a living hell and was incapable of bonding with my son.

The wounds festered

"I have to keep putting off my dreams, but you get to chase yours!"

My wife screamed these words at me when the pregnancy test for our second child came back positive.

It was early February 2013. We had been married for four years, and Judy had already paused achieving her bachelor's degree three times: once for our wedding, another time to focus on our marriage, and a third time to focus on our daughter. She had put off her dream multiple times to focus on our family, and she did not want to do it again.

On the surface it would seem like Judy was hurt because she was putting off her dream *again*. Deep down, this situation compounded with unresolved hurts in our marriage and led to new hurts, too.

Here's how it compounded on previous wounds.

For the first three years of our marriage, she had to be the stable one emotionally, spiritually, and financially. I would take my pain out on her and did not prioritize her desires and feelings. I did not show her that she was a priority, she was not safe with me, and she could not count on me for even basic marital things. My sex drive was wrecked; I was all but impotent, and I could not show her passion or desire.

As if this wasn't enough, she watched me love, prioritize, and do right for others. I was capable of great patience and affection for everyone else in my life except her. I could show others passion, prioritize their needs, be available for them at the drop of a dime, and I made damn sure to earn their trust and make sure they knew, every single time, that they were wanted and valuable.

I was living as a badass husband for everyone but my wife and my selfishness created a world of pain for her to live in.

Here is how that situation created more wounds for all of us.

Judy had finally hit a breaking point. She went into survival mode in our marriage, which meant hardening her heart against me because she could not trust me.

I was angry with her about her misperception, only focusing on that the sex was consensual and not caring that, because I didn't listen, she had to put her dreams off for the fourth time. In my anger, my self-pity spiked, as well as my attachment to my position in the church.

I went hard in the paint, hating myself, and I walled up against my own family out of shame.

One day, there were young adults from our church babysitting my daughter, and when I got home, I walked past my daughter to hug the young adults I felt so important to. The image of Amara's toddler arms lifting up to me, confused as I hugged and greeted other people first, is burned into my memory. I knew instantly that I had ignored my daughter, but it took a couple of weeks for me to care. I feel so much humiliation writing this, but us dads have got to get real about all the times we cared more for stupid things and temporary people than our own children.

I barely made eye contact with my son for the first three months of his life. I didn't cuddle him, embrace him, or see him as much more than a chore. In fact, I saw him as a chore. I took care of him, fed him, and made sure his diapers were clean and he was safe, but I was not in love with or bonded with him. From the day he was born I knew I resented him and was avoiding a connection. I was aware of it, but I was so ashamed because of it that I kept hiding from it.

I don't know how to be a man; how can I raise one?

How can I fix this issue with Judy?

How can I stop pushing Amara away?

What if Garrett becomes gay?

What if the people find out what's going on?

Why is Judy even married to me?

When will this ever end?

My entire life boiled down to compensating with my position, staying as busy as possible outside the home as I could, and asking question after question after tormenting question. My shame overwhelmed me, and I could no longer hide from it.

And I still asked, *Why can't I change?*

One day I was cuddling with Amara as Garrett sat next to us, and my indifference toward a relationship with him hit me.

I let my pain rob him of his dad.

I was disgusted at my self-pity, tired of my nonsense. I was asking myself these questions but refused to answer them.

So I did what I knew to do: own it and get help. I spoke with one of the leaders in our church, Penny Leon. She told me that if I won their hearts, they would follow me. "Win their hearts, Greg. And they will follow you."

The full weight of my fractured home hit me. I failed to win my wife's heart because I didn't know how to develop myself in the midst of my pain, and it put the burden of leadership on her. I failed to win my daughter's heart because I needed validation so much that I prioritized the people who gave me that validation, even though they were outside the home. I failed to win my son's heart because I allowed the voids in my identity as a man to dictate my behavior and pulled away from him because I was telling myself I was not good enough.

And there, on the edge of divorce, suicide, and humiliation, everything came together. The culmination of my struggle was now real, and the course of the rest of my life was secured.

I did not become the inspiring, passionate husband and father I am now by accident, and this is why you have to listen.

The abuse and trauma of my childhood made me insecure and needing validation. My insecurity hit hardest at home, inhibiting me from bonding with my wife. My position in the church and community gave me the strongest sense of worth and validation I had ever known, and I sacrificed my family to keep it. This instilled insecurity and unmet needs in my wife and kids, and they were on the course of growing up with the wounds in my heart I was failing to address. I had become worse than the people who hurt me because I knew better, and I was letting it happen.

Judy, Sissy, and Bears didn't need me to be a "good" Christian, to be a good leader at Church, to do well in college. Judy did not need another male role model, my *want* for change, or me beating myself up. Amara didn't need me to improve at public speaking or to be chosen for more mission trips. Garrett didn't need me to be a dad to other young men, read more books, or get faster. They just needed *me*.

This ties back to rule 2, accepting that I am loved. I didn't believe I was loved, so I could not receive love from my wife, so I got validation from outside the home, and this created a block in my marriage. You have to learn this.

Own everything.

Own everything. You are a dad, a man. Nothing can happen in your family and home that you do not allow. Nothing. Everything is your fault. If you think your wife's behavior is the fault of her dad or someone and not the direction you have tolerated, you are wrong. If you think your kids are behaving on some hereditary program, you are an idiot.

You are the leader. Period.

Wife has a crappy attitude? Kids aren't listening? No one believes in you? They're being mean to each other? Your kids are using harsh words toward themselves?

What needs of theirs are you ignoring? Are you focusing more on rules than on relationships? Are you defending yourself when they confront you? Are you punishing mistakes? How few promises are you keeping to yourself? Are you keeping your discipline? How are you slacking, having a crappy attitude, not listening, being mean, or using a harsh tone?

Discipline yourself to take everything happening with your wife and kids as them following your example. Look at everything they are doing as a reflection of your own behavior, attitude, thoughts, private life, discipline, morals, and character.

How did you set the example for it or allow an environment where that was tolerated?

When you run your life by combining this and rule 2, you become unstoppable. You become impervious to shame and capable of swift, powerful change.

———

APPLY THIS TODAY

1. Make note of each flaw, issue, or poor decision loop happening for your wife and kids. Get in a motivated

———

state of mind and compare what they are doing to your own conduct.

2. Whenever your family is being bad, weak, or troublesome, immediately ask yourself: *How have I taught them this?*

Turn apologizing into a skill

Not "sorry." Sorry is worthless. We are talking about owning your nonsense and leadership with passion and communicating that with such clarity that they know they are not responsible for your issues and that you are going to change.

Gone are the days when a dad could lose his temper and not own it. You don't get a pass to be an A-hole just because you worked all day.

You cannot allow your children to assume that any flaw of yours is their fault, period. Losing your temper, exceptions to the rules for you and not them, overreacting, anything.

Do not allow your children to wonder if your anger, outbursts, or hypocrisy is somehow their fault. You cannot allow even one inch of the doubt for this.

———

APPLY THIS TODAY

1. Tell your wife and kids how your decisions have set an example that they are following, and ask them to forgive you for it. *This is my fault. I have not been keeping my own*

discipline, so, of course, you are struggling with it.

2. Communicate clearly that you screwed up. Tell them how you messed up, that it was not at all their fault, and ask them to forgive you. Using an example of being stressed with work and losing your temper:

   a. *I yelled at you, but I should not have. I am stressed with work and did not handle what you did well. My yelling had nothing to do with you. Will you please forgive me?*

Adventure, Challenge, and Risk

Show your children and yourself that you are worth following. Adventure is hands down the greatest fatherhood tool. My kids have learned more about communication during Indian runs, and I have learned more about leadership doing 75 Hard with my 10-year-old. Together, we get out of the house, out of our heads, and into the moment, creating memories together.

———

APPLY THIS TODAY

1. Work out at least three times each week with them.
2. Find a rule to allow your kids to break, but only with you if they choose to. Example: I allowed my kids to start cussing at a young age. They knew they'd get in trouble cussing with others, so we had a taboo, but not immoral, thing to share. They felt cool and distinguished, and it became an enjoyable time for us.

———

    a.   Waking my daughter up in the middle of the night to sneak Oreos...

    b.   Taking my son beyond the "Do Not Enter" signs in all sorts of places...

    c.   Going for a Father-Daughter ball and sneaking into the back part of the hotel with my daughter...

3.   Expose them to risk through adventure. Risk forces your kids to look to you for guidance and forces you to make the right call. Your kids looking to you builds their trust in you, and them looking to you in combination with you making good calls boosts your confidence. Do not take them places you are not ready or equipped for.

4.   Complete frequent challenges with them. Shared hardship is a psychological tactic for building and keeping strong relationships. It forces you out of your head and into the moment and gives you clarity and control.

Fix Your Marriage

Being a great dad means you must first be a great husband.

There is no exception to this rule. You cannot allow your marriage to slip because you are focused more on the kids. The priority of promises starts with your wife, and to ensure negative cycles stay broken, noble legacies are formed, and your children have the best foundation for an incredible life, you must have a strong marriage.

Our sons and daughters base their identity and their future relationships on the example we give them through our own marriage.

APPLY THIS TODAY

1. Love your wife passionately. Any blockage to this needs to be attacked immediately.
2. Schedule time for your wife that the children are not allowed to interrupt, and make sure this time takes place on a weekly basis.
3. Fix your marriage. Stop feeling sorry for yourself and blaming her. You're the man. Get the help you both need and make it right.
4. Be patient, kind, supportive, and thankful for her, and let your children see you express it.

DEBRIEF - WIN THEIR HEARTS

- Dads, your family will only go in the direction you choose through your daily life. If you do not pick a direction and live it all the way, your family will be shaped by whatever impulse or pain or feeling you have. It all starts with you.

- No matter how things have been, you can start winning their hearts right now by working to bond, owning your crap, and getting better at apologizing.

- If you win their hearts, they will follow you. Do the work to be a man worth following, and see what is possible when your family trusts you!

- To win their hearts, you must first win your own, and this can only be accomplished by you becoming the dad you admire mentally, physically, emotionally, and spiritually.

- If you think you can shortcut this section, go back to Chapter III (5 Emasculations).

PART IV:
EPILOGUE

XVIII
WHAT ARE YOU GOING TO DO ABOUT IT?

Say a prayer for the pretender. Who started out
so young and strong, only to surrender.
– Jackson Browne, The Pretender

Dads, brothers, moms, and everyone else - thank you for joining me on this journey. For years, I have imagined this moment, having compiled my story and experience into a consumable format to hopefully impact the lives of others.

For your time, attention, and purchase, thank you.

This Is Only The Beginning

These nine principles are only the start. We could write more books than the world has room for on how to truly conquer darkness, stop negative family cycles, and positively impact our families.

I was tempted to expound on this journey with a myriad of

other stories, strategies, and actions. I left the book as it is, with these nine rules, because these are the ones that will lead you to every other thing.

Loving regret will help you make better decisions for your health and time.

Carrying a worthy burden will help you find optimism and positivity in darkness.

Controlling your thoughts and processing fear and negative self-talk will help you better and more quickly identify root issues.

Connecting with good noble men as part of your discipline will help you clarify the negative patterns that you are called to break for your family.

EFT will force you to admit your limits and give you the humility you will need to get the right help and do something with it.

Receiving love will soften the parts of your heart that should not harden, compelling you to love with greater passion and forgive those who hurt you.

Everything is connected, and excellence is a transferable skill, even when it comes to quality of life.

Pursuing the impossible

We have an impossible standard, dads. To be everything they

need and nothing they do not. To lead from the front and exemplify with true integrity what we want for and from our family.

You and I both know there isn't a perfect father in the world except for God. After all of my experience, success, victory, and teaching, even I fail hard. In fact, 10 minutes ago, I went downstairs to check on my children and was not fully engaged in their questions and discourse because my mind was preoccupied with the stress of my current goals and circumstances.

You and I will do amazing things, and our children will still need help and healing from something we could have done better, done more, or not done at all.

There is no escaping it because we live in a fallen world.

The standard is impossible but not unreachable. We can fall and still be amazing.

Using my failure from a few moments ago, my kids still wanted affection and showed love to me. Why? Because I keep chasing the standard. I keep getting back up and working to be a dad I admire, and they see it. There are pains and sins from my family that will not pass on to my kids because of me. That is worth noting.

And it is worth fighting for. From now on, say to yourself "LINEAGE" every time you think about being a father. You and I have the power to shape things for people who aren't even born yet, and that really is worth dying for.

Perfection is the idea, but the pursuit of it is the goal. Brother, you cannot pursue perfection correctly if you use all of your failures to beat yourself over the head. Have some damn grace for yourself, and go try again.

Get it right more than you don't. Follow these nine rules and let the majority of your life be shaped by them. And don't stop.

There is no finish line.

ACKNOWLEDGMENTS:
A DEBT OF GRATITUDE
—

Remembering those without whom I would have never made it.

Amara, Garrett, this list is not even close to complete. Do not forget the people who helped you.

The point is to honor them in permanent writing and to remember that no person makes it alone. I have gone far because I went with people. I was willing to shut up and learn and got good at asking for help from the right people.

Judy Wanberg: As of writing this, we have been married for 5,407 days. You are the only woman who was able to truly keep up. You are an absolute savage. You married me because you knew that, no matter what, at the end of the day, I'd do the right thing. You knew me to be a man after God's heart. You were right, and I will love you forever.

Nathan Sandford: You showed me that my life was worth living. Telling me about the call on my life and not letting me forget who I am. Giving me a position to develop my gifts and leadership. Fathering me. You were the first person in my life brave enough to cut through my issues and reach me. Thank you.

Loren Sandford: You were a father to me. Teaching me to embrace pain. Not allowing me to take shortcuts. Teaching me that those who shrink back at every difficulty don't have the strength for more. To love pragmatism. You encouraged me to put the ranger away and I think I finally get it. I'll see you soon.

Beth Sandford: You embodied rule 2 and held us accountable to it. Thank you.

Mindy Sandford: Your believing in me made me feel really good about myself. We are akin to one another in the scars we have. Don't give up.

Luke Himes: My first best friend. Echo Lake and drifting in the Honda. You are the hardest working man I ever met. Also, sorry again about knocking the bumper off.

Mike Dudley: You are my best friend. You helped me be who I am today. I wanted to be your friend so badly, but I was embarrassed at how much I complained about what I was going through. So, I pretended to be better than I was and only talked about the good stuff, and turns out that was what I needed the whole time. You challenged me on how little I thought of myself with the low-paying jobs and even kicked my butt when I refused to change. In the midst of that horrible seven years, I talked about the same problem on two separate occasions, and you called me on it: "We talked about this same thing three weeks ago. Why are we still talking about it?" Thank you for holding me accountable for my thoughts.

Dad: You were there every time you said you would be. We have bonded again. Even later in life, you decided to change to support me. I love you.

Mom: One day, you will know how perfectly God loves you and how fervently I hoped for you. I pray for you always. Go in peace.

Julie & Jay: You played one of the most significant roles in my life. You became the parents I needed and helped me stay on the course long enough for it to solidify. I definitely sped in the van more than I told you, but you knew anyway. Thank you for giving me a chance, standing by my side for multiple demonic deliverances, supporting me financially while I was in India, and loving my wife and kids. I hope you dust off your passion and keep running this race well.

Paul Baneta: My brother in India, you edified me about my hunger for righteousness, which helped me see who I truly was. I miss you. Thank you for being a friend and older brother while I worked under you in India. You are a good man. I love you.

Devin Wanberg: You took me to church that night I stole drugs and got kicked out of the home. You taught me to sacrifice the lesser for the greater and how to kill desire until it was truly dead so I could be obedient to God. Thank you.

Cody Wanberg: Little brother, you have been a pillar of wisdom in my life since the beginning. I love who you are. Thank you for always caring about me and leaving me with clarity every single time we talk.

John Grdina: You helped me learn more about the gifts and abilities God gave me. You helped me to identify other pitfalls and dead ends I was committing myself to out of misplaced notions of loyalty. I love you, brother. Thank you.

Edgar: We have not known each other long, but I respect you tremendously. Thank you for not compromising on the faith or your family despite being an incredibly dangerous man.

Justin Shealey: You are one of the best leaders I know. Thank you for always just wanting to help. I love you, brother.

Grandma Shirley: I want to apologize for how I let my shame keep me away. You kept loving me and I would forget to call, but you didn't care. You were just so proud of the man I had become. I will miss our time doing puzzles, yard work, putting TV stands and furniture together. You edified my love for work and inspired me to look beyond what was plainly visible. Thank you for loving me. I hope you went home.

Grandpa Wanberg: You fed my love for poetry and stoicism and edified my proclivity for looking beyond what was visible to find powerful ideals.

Jesse Keeney: You are a little brother to me, always. You are my wise counsel. Thank you for never forgetting the Lord and for not letting me forget who I am, either.

Chris Gagliardi: You are the friend who followed me into the wild. Camping at Timberline in the winter, doing a Murph without preparing, disappearing for a weekend to reset and focus: you were always down. Thank you for being an uncle to my children and for not giving up on yourself. Now, go get

---

your woman;).

Trisha Frost: Jack's teaching on the Taskmasters is what started the seven years of what the world would call "psychosis." Writing this book compelled me to reach out. Even though we met later in both our lives, it was impactful. You helped bring deeper healing to ungodly beliefs that I would always be poor and would succeed less despite hard work. Thank you for taking time to be with me.

Collin & Katie Wanberg

Dylan & Jessica Wanberg

Matt & Lynette Hoyle

Fred & Elizabeth Hoon

Jordan & Andra Johnson

Jordon & Rhea DoRito

Bill & Charity Delude

Bill & Penny Leon

Joe & Dave Wright

Jeanette Flores (formerly Coash)

John Martin (Men In The Frey)

Mike & Samantha Pike

Mark & Connie Vanderstoep

Mike & Jan Barnes

Josh & Jenn DeLong

The Maroney's

Sgt. Graham Dunne

Gabe Alexander

Armed & Dadly (Eric Portwood)

Becky Cox

Steve Eckert

Josh Flores

Maggi Flores

Jacob Flores

Patrick, Joe, Ben Maroney

Mike Simonton

WHAT ARE YOU GOING TO DO ABOUT IT?

Inspiration is wasted if it doesn't drive action.

My favorite question: what are you going to do about it?

There is a massive need for male role models, to bypass many of the obstacles and get results. I believe everyone should have a coach. I have been under constant mentorship by at least one person at a time for more than 21 years.

But for dads like you and me, who came from broken homes and need guidance *and* help at our core, more than a coach is needed.

This is why I have given my life to helping dads. This is why I created a private community of men. This is why I developed Signal Fire, a 6 month 1-on-1 coaching program. I want to help dads be the legacy-minded leader they needed so they can:

- Get control of their thoughts and emotions

- Have a sense of worth

- Be *the* respected leader of their home

- Increase their sex drive

- Meet high demands of fatherhood with excellence

- Live inside their mind with valor

- Make better money

- Turn their pain into purpose

The door between you now and you being the hero for your family is an irrevocable commitment to investing in a mentor and a community.

If I can do this for you, get in touch with me.

ABOUT THE AUTHOR

Greg Wanberg is the motivator for dads from broken homes and has served as a mentor and coach for over two decades. Having overcome addiction and depression and endured trauma, Greg helps fathers exceed the high demands of fatherhood and overcome depression without years of therapy or medication. Greg serves his community in uniform as a firefighter.

He lives in South Carolina with his wife and children, where he enjoys shooting, hiking, practicing self-defense, and learning land navigation.

Greg can be contacted for speaking engagements and media request at: **contact@gregwanberg.com**

He can also be found on Instagram **@greg.wanberg** sharing his message of accountability and hope.